"More than ever, the challenges we face in our lives and in the world can feel enormous, and people are seeking help to heal and to live fully. In this beautifully written book, you'll get so many priceless insights from a brilliant man who has spent his life being of service to others, finding practical solutions to challenges great and small. Larry takes us into the realm of 'putting things right', using not only physical tools, but even more powerful tools like creativity, perspective, and love. What I love best is that the life-changing wisdom here is given amidst stories from Larry's life, combined with his dry humor, so it's fun to read. Whether you feel anything in your life needs 'fixing' now or not, this book is a delightful gift that you can give yourself and to those you love!"

–Dr. Clint G. Rogers, author of Ancient Secrets of a Master Healer

The *Philosopher's* Wrench

BOOK ONE

The *Philosopher's* Wrench

BOOK ONE

Using Your Creativity,
Heart & Tools
to Fix the World

Larry Weingarten

Published by Wisdom of the World Press

ISBN (paperback): 978-1-952353-97-0
ISBN (ebook): 978-1-952353-96-3

Book design: Christy Day, Constellation Book Services

Printed in the United States of America

Dedication

This book I dedicated to all those who have lit my path. To my mentors, family, and chosen family who have taken the time and gone out of their way to make me a better and more useful person. Now, I get to pass along their gifts.

Contents

Is this a do-it-yourself book?

Although many of the procedures I discuss are of the do-it-yourself variety, some are not. They require professional plumbing or electrical skills. If you don't possess the needed tools or skills, it's essential for safety that you get qualified help. As the reader, your advantage will lie in knowing exactly what you want to have done. Likewise, I'm not a therapist, counselor, money manager, or prophet! Getting qualified help where needed is key. I cannot be responsible for any damage caused by the use or misuse of information in this book.

Foreword by Dan Holohan

If you're lucky in life, you'll occasionally have a conversation with someone that will stay with you forever. Maybe it was something your spouse said when you least expected it. Or perhaps it was your child showing you a reflection of the sky in a puddle after a storm. She may have told you that when it rains, some of the sky goes into the ground. She'll point at the puddle and tell you to look. Look! It's right there! And if you're lucky in life you will take the time to look. And when you do, you'll see the beauty that is in your child and in the entire world if you just take the time to look for it.

Larry Weingarten has written a book that takes the time to really look for that beauty. His book is unusual as it weaves together the mechanical and the soulful; the playful and the practical. In it you'll learn a lot about pipes, and heaters, and the water that makes up most of our planet here, but there's much more to consider along the way. Watch a sunset, pet cats, or ponder the meaning of life. Savor this beautiful book. It will make you think. It will make you remember. It will make you consider what it is to be truly human.

Larry was visiting from California a few years ago. We have been friends for a long time, and now we are also Brothers, through our membership in The General Society of Mechanics and Tradesmen of the City of New York, founded in 1785. Larry was in New York because he had just donated nearly his entire collection of antique water heaters to the Mechanics Institute, which is a part of The General Society. Mechanics Institute has offered tuition-free, two- and three-year nightly schooling to the trades since 1858. It resides in The General Society's landmarked building at 20 West 44th Street in Manhattan.

We were sitting on my patio, sipping wine and talking about life. Larry is the gentlest person I have ever known. He smiles quietly and always pauses before he speaks. I had noticed that about him since we first met, but it was only on that day that I asked him why he does that.

"Before I answer anyone, anyone at all," he said, "I always ask myself whether what I'm about to say will help."

I sat with that thought for a long moment, and waited.

"And what if you decide that it won't help?" I said.

And there was that quiet smile again. "Then I don't say it," Larry said. "It won't help if I do say it, so I try to think of something to say that will help. Often that's a matter of turning things around a bit. I have to think before I speak. So I pause."

That made me pause. I paused for a good long while. I thought about the many times in my life when I had shot back with a too-quick answer to someone's question because I was annoyed, or busy doing other things, or just felt like being snide at that moment because I thought the other person's question was stupid. And I know the old saw about there being no such thing as a stupid question, but not everyone sees things that way.

I'm retired now but I made my living as an author and speaker in the heating industry. A homeowner once asked me if it was okay to use gasoline in an oil burner if he ran out of fuel oil. "I mean only in an emergency," he said.

BL (Before Larry), I probably would have asked the homeowner if he was out of his mind. Did he want to kill his entire family? How could he ask such a stupid question?!

But then I remembered that one of Larry's donated antique water heaters, a very old one, did indeed burn gasoline, so I know it can be done. But I also know that modern oil burners burn oil and not gasoline. And if you try to burn gasoline, you're also going to burn down your house. So I gently explained that to the homeowner. I paused first, of course.

Will it help?

That simple question stays with me now. It haunts me because it makes me reflect on so many times when I didn't take a moment to ask myself that simple question. But that was BL.

Larry knows stuff and he knows how to fix things. He knows more about water heaters than anyone else I have ever met in more than 50 years in this business. He knew when it was time to donate his water-heater collection because he knew that the Mechanics Institute would use it as a teaching tool for as long as there is a New York City. It will outlive us all. That is selfless thinking, and that is beautiful.

Larry knows stuff and he knows how to build things. He once showed me a cardboard model of a house he wanted to someday live in. And then he built that house, all by himself. He also built the road leading up to that house at the highest point on a California hill. That house has all the modern conveniences, and it is disconnected from the grid. Larry used old books to get many of the ideas that went into that house. Many minds went into the planning. Most whispered from the yellowed pages of those old books. This house sips energy and he calls it Hummingbird Hill because that's where the hummingbirds gather each day. Some sit on his finger because he feeds them and because he is gentle person. Other wild beasties—bobcats and deer and rabbits and others—also visit with Larry each day. He sits with them. He communicates with them all. I've seen him do it. It made my spirit quiet, watching him. Shh. Listen. Hear it?

Larry is kind. He reads widely. He explains himself with words that soar, but are easy to follow. Soar with them. He writes here in small, delicious portions. Begin where you will. This book is a buffet of thoughts about water, about heating water, about plumbing, but mostly it is a book about what it means to be still, what it means to be human, what it means to see the sky in a puddle and smile at the beauty of it all.

Larry Weingarten, my dear friend and Brother, has written a gorgeous book. Savor it. You'll learn about plumbing and water heating here, and you'll also learn about life.

Will it help?
Yes, it will.

Guiding Lights

Scattered throughout this book are little guiding lights. When you see that lighthouse symbol, there will be a "rule" that I try to live by, or at least keep in mind. In my life, these guiding lights help me make decisions about tricky situations, or know what direction to take. Maybe you'll have use for some of them too, or even add some of your own.

Preface

On Writing

It's as though there are lots of critters in my head and they want out! They are mostly benign creatures…sort of warm, eager, and fuzzy. Fuzzy because they are behind a thin veil, so are hard to see well, but they really want to come out and play. They want to be seen clearly and interact with others, too. Well, some of them also have a message they feel is important to share. In lieu of critters, they could be called ideas, thoughts, or feelings. Heck, maybe some of them are notions or even crazy suppositions. You get to decide. Whatever you call them, they have been quietly collecting in my brain and heart for a long time. Now they want out so that they may be seen, considered, hopefully accepted, and grow happily in other minds and hearts. If I have done a good job of writing them down, they will be easy for you to see…clearly! That's important to them, because fuzzy just doesn't do when the message really wants to be clear. The critters simply want to help in whatever way works. They may inspire, help you to see a different perspective, make your heart glow a bit, or help you to uncover your own critters deep inside that also want to be heard, seen, and shared. Maybe my critters will make a trail that your critters will turn into a road! Think of all those happy and productive critters!

Let's think of just one of the critters as an example. The word timshel has played a large role in my life. I first encountered it in the book by John Steinbeck, *East of Eden*. The definition of that word, to me, is, "You have a choice. You always have a choice."

Think about that for a bit. It turns every roadblock into an opportunity to find another, better way; to get as creative as you are able and to go places other people sometimes have trouble even imagining. It allows you to turn what others call pain into a path for greater understanding. It lets you see others with an open mind and heart. And it abolishes fear! Now isn't that a nice critter to have close by? That's why the critters really want to be clearly seen. They can make our lives and all lives we touch better, but only if we're aware of them. So, come meet my critters! With a little investment of time, they can become your furry friends, as well.

This book is a collection of various things; many are short musings, others longer reflections, and others just interesting technical stuff. You can read the book from front to back, or you can drift around in it at random. If you're looking for insights about specific technical issues, check out the sections on Hot Water/Energy, Plumbing, and Housing; you might learn some useful tidbits about a passion of mine, hot water. If you're interested in housing, I've got some thoughts for you! Or my interest in making things very energy-efficient might stand out. Then have a look through the philosophical chapters. Perhaps you'll see the concept and power of "perspective" in a whole new light. Maybe my respect for and love of animals will rub you the right way. You'll notice that there is an animal story at the end of most sections. To me, they are a unifying force. Whatever you find in these words that strikes a chord with you, I hope it helps you feel more connected with this magnificent world—or, at a minimum, better able to confidently deal with plumbing problems. Then you'll see "Living World," "Out There," and "Realities," which I hope you'll find interesting and just possibly fun. Maybe you'll find new perspectives to consider and explore further.

My hope is that these writings—technical, philosophical, and the merger of both—will empower you and make it easier for you to live life just as you want to!

Introduction

This book is about fixing things...all sorts of things! Also, it's about seeing the world in a slightly different way. In it, I merge the worlds of technology and philosophy, which we have been taught to believe have no relation to each other. One uses your hands and the other uses your brain. But the end product of mixing both worlds is something richer than either can offer. After all, in our bodies the hands and brain are well connected, along with the heart! The process of fixing physical things is remarkably similar to the process of fixing emotional and spiritual issues. Enlisting the powers of openness, perspective, and a quiet mind can go far in helping you fix any sort of problem that crosses your path or that you may have been burdened with. This understanding and confidence these powers bring is truly life-changing! Imagine a life with no real fears; imagine the calmness you would feel.

This book is a series of essays on a wide range of topics, from fixing your water heater and good housing, to traveling in time and space, to relating to our world with all of its inhabitants, to seeing everything more deeply. The goal is to uncover those truths hidden in plain sight. A bit of humor in these pages should help the messages taste better, too!

I've been in the trades since I was a teenager, and have now spent over fifty years working with my hands—and at times my brain. These days, I'm regarded as an expert on hot water, energy, and building science. I've written for trade journals and consulted with people all over the world about these things. I was even written up in the *New York Times* for a very energy efficient off-grid home I designed and built. Thirty years ago, I wrote an entire book on how to maintain water heaters. It's surprising how many areas of our lives, energy, hot water, and building science touches. We stand to gain a **lot** by understanding and utilizing this science in a better way.

Even way back in grade school, I was the one teachers called on to fix things or modify them to suit their needs. "The alarm bell is too loud."

"Okay, I have some ideas."

"Larry, the heater isn't keeping the room warm."

"Let me have a look."

While other kids were on the playground, I got to have even more fun messing with equipment. Some teachers understood and actually appreciated my different-ness.

My high school English teacher was one of those observant and trusting souls. Back when I was his student, he wanted a lie detector so that students wouldn't even try to cheat on tests. I put together a motorized thingy in a wooden cigar box with flashing lights. When he was going to give a test, he'd bring it out where all could see—and apparently it worked. The students didn't want to take a chance that it might be real!

I've found that the path of life can be a bit rocky, and there are times when you just don't know which way to turn. I've had my share of those times—and have grown because of them. Luckily, I've had good mentors share their perspectives with me at the right times. They taught me some wonderful lessons! I decided to write down some stories, observations, and ways of being that have helped me get over the bumps in the road of life. Fast-forward fifty years to a recent conversation with that same English teacher—who's still a good friend. He took a look at some of my scribbles and said, "You must publish this!"

So now you're holding those scribbles. I believe that everyone has experiences in life, along with those a-ha moments that can be useful to others, and those are best shared. There is something about being of service to others that's just magnificent. I've been able to save lives from both dangerous equipment and suicide. To me, it's the apex of feeling useful.

Because I'm a hands-on sort, I have included some technical stuff I've learned over the years that can be useful in an immediate and practical way. I've given information that can help you keep your water heater from blowing up or causing fires or spewing carbon monoxide. That could keep you out of the news in a good way! Energy efficiency is a passion of mine also, so you'll find pointers about how to look at and deal with the big, wide realm of energy use in buildings, from how to make plumbing much more water and energy efficient to making your home more durable, which is a facet of efficiency.

Once I started thinking about how to be more helpful than is possible with technical information alone, the floodgates just opened up! These essays come from all over the place. They are stories, observations, truths, and even one where I was simply the conduit. The words and attitudes weren't even mine. Sometimes I didn't even know why I was taking time to write, but just did it so that particular nugget wouldn't be lost. I let the child in me take over sometimes. Why not?

I've seen so much pain and unnecessary sadness caused by not making time to understand that I thought I'd try to write bite-sized pieces about things in my own life that have helped or been important to me. I believe they can be of service to you, too. Here you can get nearly instant gratification with technical things, peace that comes from being rid of fear, and that warmth that happens when you accept and relate to all of the life around you. Even flights of fancy can be a good massage for the mind. I'll be bold and say it directly, there is wisdom gathered here for you to drink from. Enjoy! ☺

 Work in a way that benefits all life.

You live in a community.

Practical Philosophy

Thoughts on Having a Second Childhood

As I get older, I'm having second thoughts about the concept of having a "second" childhood. Think about what you just loved as a kid. Now think about your motivations and needs as a grownup. Did things really change? Yeah sure, you probably added pressing things like taking care of your kids or your parents. Earning a living probably became important, too.

I was raised under the concept that childhood ends at some point, and adulthood begins. It carries responsibilities, like putting your own desires on the back burner in order to take care of others, and to properly manage your affairs. I was shown that adulthood meant being mostly serious instead of playful. One definition of adult is to "behave in a way characteristic of a responsible adult, especially by accomplishing mundane but necessary tasks."

But did those things you loved as a child simply fade away, or did they help guide you in quiet ways? If you just couldn't wait to go walking in the woods as a child, don't you still find ways to be in or near the forest? As a child, I felt a magnetic pull toward the water. That never left. When I was too busy earning a living to actually get to the water, I still kept the water in sight nearly every day and nurtured my memories of being near, on, and under it.

Cats can provide some perspective here. I've raised feral cats, shelter cats, and cats from litters at other households. Some I got as tiny kittens, and they needed bottle feeding. The cats I got really young never changed. Their personality as small kittens remained constant through the years. If a kitten was the boss and unafraid of things, so was the cat. It's been fun to see!

So I wonder if people have traits that stick with them, just like cats have. Although we can learn new ways of behaving, it seems to me that we're pretty consistent. If you were shy as a child, you may be able to come across as a bold adult, but that shyness probably still exists inside. In short, there's a good chance that whatever you were driven by as a child probably still exists within you. If so, then the "second childhood" phase just means letting your kid come out and play again instead of being kept bottled up.

I actively go looking for things that would have made my kid-self happy. I now make time to visit the water with all of its life and smells, relishing the little joyful moments. Or sometimes I sit quietly and just enjoy the many nuances of being in the forest, just as I did when first learning about it years ago. I'm still busy with a bit too much to do, but the tranquility that comes with letting myself be a kid again is absolutely worth the time spent. Spending some time in these environments, which are so full of life makes me a richer person in ways more important than dollars. Living in a childlike way lets me be present in the "right now" and experience things I'd otherwise miss.

So, I'm questioning the concept of second childhood. I imagine childhood actually never left, but simply was waiting for me to let it come out and play—to see more clearly with all my senses the grand, exciting, intriguing world that we're part of.

What and Where is Comfort?

Comfort is an interesting thing. When I think of the word, being physically comfortable is the first thing that comes to my mind. But it seems there are many forms of comfort, and once you've named them it's easier to get them back if they're missing from your life. So, let's identify some sources of comfort.

Sometimes comfort comes from just keeping some emotional or physical distance from people or situations that steal your tranquility and comfort. You know who I'm talking about. It's that "friend" or relative who just has to correct you or find fault much of the time. And that brings up another form of comfort: remembering that the choice is always yours; you are not trapped, and you don't have to give up your power to others.

Being surrounded by things you know, particularly things that have stories that may go back generations, can be comforting, as well. I built a nook in my living room where I display mementos that go back to my great-great-grandparents. When I sit with these, each one quietly tells me its stories; I never get tired of doing this. I find that the silent comfort of sitting with my ancestors is made even better by having a cat in my lap.

A very different form of comfort is knowing how to deal with physical things, or knowing trustworthy people you can call. I can fix most things that go wrong in buildings, so I have nothing to worry about in that arena. And I know a guy who's great with numbers and another who's good with cars, and yet another who enjoys the digital world. I don't have to worry about these areas, as these friends all keep me comfortably on track.

I also find comfort in having good friends. Isn't it nice to know there are people in your world who will pick up the phone when you call? Isn't it a great feeling knowing that others have your back? A little story: I was staying at a friend's house far from my home for what was supposed to be one night. While there, I became painfully ill. My friend and his wife hunted down the treatment I needed and tended to me for another two days while I healed. They didn't have to do that, but they made me and my care their top priority. And they are busy people! I felt **so** blessed. They absolutely had my back, and I'll have theirs whenever they need me.

In these times, when truth can seem very slippery, just knowing your foundations and knowing they are unshakeable can be another big source of comfort. Some things are true no matter what. Will the sun rise? **Yes!** Do the points of the compass change? Not very fast. Will that pet you raised from a pup or kitten want to be near you? Yup! Change is a constant in our world, but fortunately, there are many truths you can rely on to carry you through difficult times. What truths are foundational for you?

Good health is another comfort that rises to the top for me—more so as I get older! Too many of my friends have died from cancer or other diseases that modern medicine didn't know how to deal with. So, part of my comfort comes from learning about ancient systems of healing that can offer help when Western medicine falls short. In particular, the ancient Indian and Chinese healing modalities can work well with chronic conditions that Western medicine can't cure.

Finally, back to the obvious one: physical comfort. Feeling the warmth of sunlight on my skin on a slightly cool day…Getting the shower temperature and force just right…Having no real aches, pains, or itches—just being undistracted by those things so that I can enjoy whatever I'm doing. Because our bodies are usually with us wherever we go, physical comfort is basic to enjoying all the other comforts.

Much of what I've talked about here could be described in other ways. It could be called satisfaction, education, or simply peace. It's waiting for us around nearly every corner. Think of the things in your life that are constant irritants, imbalances, unfair, or just wrong. Every one of them can be dealt with. One approach is to fix what is in your power to fix and don't spend another drop of energy on what's beyond your power to improve. And after doing all that work, take a day off and get comfortable at your favorite spa!

Hidden Strengths

I recently finished teaching a class of about fifty maintenance workers on some of the nuances of water heater repair —and in the process I learned something about my source of strength.

We were playing with some long-dead water heaters that had been captured on their way to the dump. I like using old water heaters as a teaching tool; they have stories to tell about their lives if you know how to look. In that exercise, we were removing pipe nipples from the tops of the heaters. Some were rather stuck!

A few students said, "This is too hard. I can't do water heater maintenance."

I don't like the word "can't," so I jumped in to see if this old white-haired guy could make the stubborn pipe nipple move. I put my trusty Hoe wrench from 1922 on the nipple and focused. The pipe came loose. Students were surprised!

It happened again, twice. A student was unable to budge the pipe nipple (even using my wrench) and I waltzed in and made it spin. The young guys with visible muscles rippling in their arms had no success while this old guy did—what gives?

Finally, someone asked me what my trick was. I had to think for a bit, but I remembered back about fifty years when I was shown this trick by my first mentor, Mom: Face a friend and rest your hand on the friend's shoulder, with your arm straight. Have your friend put their hands above your elbow joint and try to bend your elbow downward. Resist by focusing on your arm and giving it all the strength it has, doing your best to keep your arm straight. When I first tried this, my arm bent despite my best effort. Now put your hand on your friend's shoulder again, but this time keep your arm straight while concentrating on the area just under your breastbone as your source of strength. Let your friend try to bend your arm, and see what happens this time. In my case, my Mom couldn't do it. My arm remained straight!

I'm just a plumber, and I don't know how this works, but I know that it does. Over the decades since I learned this trick, I worked it into my practice without thinking about it. It's simply that I refuse to walk away from a job without finishing it, and this "trick" has allowed me to finish every job. The guys who couldn't make the pipe nipples come loose thought I'd bested them, but the point was really that I'd demonstrated a tool we all have that most of us don't use. It sounds woo-woo, but it works.

There are a couple of other not-so-obvious tricks I've learned over the years. For example, the plumber who appears to move the slowest often gets the work done the fastest. When you go to a job, sit down and map out the work in your head before you pick up a tool. Understand every step of what you'll be doing before you start. This way, when you get going on it, things will come together smoothly and you won't need to redo anything. When you finish, it will be just as you envisioned. That feels pretty good!

Here's another trick that helps me work effectively. I've noticed that I think in pictures. When I can get a clear picture in my mind of what I'm trying to accomplish, it inevitably works. When I can only get a fuzzy image in my head, it doesn't work; I wind up needing to figure out a different way. So, on your next project, see if getting a clear picture before you start works for you. It just might save you some time and frustration.

The moral of these stories? Sometimes it's the subtle shifts in focus that make your actions powerful.

The Power of Perspective

"Perspective" is a deceptively simple word, yet there is enormous power in its application. Sometimes we have a fixed, narrow perspective: "If all you have is a hammer, everything looks like a nail."

But without multiple perspectives, one becomes stuck in only one way of seeing the world. Then everyone else becomes wrong, and the inability to agree on things and get stuff done becomes normal. And I'm not even talking about politics! Additionally, the power of having multiple perspectives is probably the finest troubleshooting tool available.

Fortunately, the more tools (perspectives) you have, the greater the odds that you will accomplish what you want to do, whatever that is. As a little thought experiment, let's take the concept of time. We all get that an hour is an hour long and a day has twenty-four of those hours (though, as I get older, years seem to get shorter). Now, what is an hour to a mayfly (an adult lives from a half hour to two weeks), or to a Giant Sequoia tree (which can live over 3,000 years)? I suspect that if the Giant Sequoia had eyes, it couldn't even blink in an hour. And what does a billion-year-old igneous rock think of the concept of an hour, or even of time itself?

Coming back to a more practical application, imagine that you're trying to fix a recalcitrant hot water system. You look at things, and all the right parts are there and seem to be working, but the system isn't working correctly. Hmmm, no clue what's wrong! Now look at the system and imagine what will happen to the various components over time. Oh, now you see that the pump will tend to freeze up with hard or gritty water. You notice de-zincification in brass valves, you find scale buildup at the mixing valve above the water heater that "sees" hot water all the time, and finally you notice rust building up at dissimilar metal connections, such as between brass pipe and steel at the tank, or dielectric unions filling with rust and restricting flow. Those are a few clues you can actually work with!

See how many more possible problems come to light with the application of just one different perspective? Now you can add the perspectives of where that hot water system lives and what conditions it experiences, both inside and outside. Imagine how the equipment might function in varying kinds of weather—hot, cold, dry, windy, wet. Think about water quality and how very hard water—or acidic or corrosive or high/low pressure water—could affect things.

You might also look at the system with different eyes—ones that see heat! These days there are inexpensive thermal cameras like the Flir One that simply plug into your cell phone and let you see even minor temperature differences. Now you can see if the pump is overheating or if the pipes that should be hot actually are. You can "look" under sinks and find cross-connections in the plumbing.

Perspective is such a useful tool! It can allow you to see things not only in different time frames, water qualities, and thermal conditions, but also through the eyes and ears of those who live with the troublesome equipment. They may respond differently than you, depending on their knowledge and comfort level with the equipment, but they live with the system and can describe just how it misbehaves. That's useful info for the troubleshooter!

Expectations can get in the way of having multiple perspectives. This is because they limit what we can take in, narrowing our vision. Have you ever had someone at a busy intersection wait for you to merge, but you missed the opportunity because you had no expectation of being shown that kindness? Having expectations is normal, but when things don't go as expected, we usually aren't too happy about it. Expectation ties in closely with judgment, which is often negative. Is it possible to go through life with fewer expectations? Perhaps a better question would be: Is it possible to suspend our expectations for a while and simply see how things play out without an emotional response? I have had to imagine I was from a different planet (particularly useful around some relatives) and just try to take in what was happening around me, rather than being frustrated or annoyed with things. It's surprising how much easier it can be to deal with people if you bring little in the way of expectations. Instead, try bringing open ears and just listen. A sense of humor doesn't hurt either. So, how do we make it easy (and fun) to get those multiple perspectives? Well, being able to tap into the wellspring of multiple perspectives probably comes from having an active imagination. Kids usually have good imaginations, and we were all kids once. Can you call up that no-holds-barred imagination when you need it? Think of it as a gift from your past. Maybe, as you grew up, you were told an active imagination was silly, or a waste of time, or just childish, but it's none of those. It's a doorway to the power of multiple perspectives.

When you were a child, just having fun imagining waving a magic wand around, or riding on your magic carpet, or spending time in your cardboard box/castle, you weren't limiting your perspectives with reality. You were giving your powerful imagination the freedom to do just what it felt like. Good troubleshooting involves thinking about all the possibilities no matter how silly they seem and then refining your thoughts with real world facts.

Perspectives arise from our experience. A seventy-year-old will have vastly different points of view than a child, yet the lucky grown-up will remember their youthful perspectives and call on them when needed. A kid who can turn into a tree or a superhero in nanoseconds is someone to appreciate, not correct.

Perspective is different than tolerance. For example, it's easy to be tolerant of someone who has suffered, but understanding their perspective requires sitting down with them and learning (and feeling) just what they've been through. Feeling others' pain isn't fun, but it will make you a more compassionate and understanding person. Perspective employs your imagination to let you see the world and its parts in a more comprehensive way. It helps you find a balance between right and wrong, pretty and ugly, confidence and fear. Perspective lets you stand back and see the contrasts and helps you to find useful lessons in those differences. All that leads to a richer life!

Teaching

I just finished up a week of teaching California State Parks maintenance folks. I know some public grade-school and junior college teachers and they are a bit jealous. It's because I get the best students! My students must compete to get into the class; they really want to learn and they bring their own experience to class for others to learn from. "Real" teachers usually have to deal with reluctant students, crowd control, and administrative headaches. I just get to share what

I've learned, which I've been doing with Parks for twenty-eight years now. They have basic, intermediate, and advanced classes in plumbing, as well as other fields. This was a basic plumbing class, with students ranging from newbies to a few who could almost have taught the class themselves.

If you step back and look at what people choose to do in their careers these days, you'll see that working in the trades is low on the list. People seem to want white-collar jobs or something to do with information technology. Across the trades, contractors are having a harder and harder time finding decent help. Yet there is a lot of work to do! Plumbing still misbehaves, buildings still need upkeep, an ever-growing number of people need a place to live, and all of the infrastructure that living in a first world country seems to require needs to be serviced. Who's gonna keep it all running?

Plumbers and electricians where I live often charge well over $100 per hour. If you become a member of one of the trade unions, you can get a good wage, decent benefits, and continuing education. We really need to rethink our push in the U.S. toward getting all students into college while forgetting about the trades. Perhaps when plumbers can charge as much as lawyers, more people will be interested in doing plumbing for a living. And plumbing is a lot less messy!

So, the question is, how do we attract people to the trades and develop a good workforce? I imagine the answer has a lot to do with how the idea of working in the trades is presented. If it's presented truthfully, showing the craft itself along with the business side, the dealing with people side, and the fact that it often has dirty, difficult, and demanding work along with very good income and the reward of helping people and sometimes keeping them from harm, it might not scare everyone away. Lots of people seem to be born with mechanical talents. They tinker with stuff as children, are inquisitive about how things work, and are quite comfortable with tools in their hands. Many have an independent streak in them, too. These people are going to be self-employed someday because they just want to do it their way, on their terms. These are the people I most want to get involved with the trades, and the best way I know to do that is by teaching. Teaching is a skill unto itself and is something I was certainly not born with.

I used to feel nothing but awkward when getting up in front of any crowd…unless it was a small crowd and I could talk about something I really knew and liked, like hot water. Nobody has asked me to give a talk on cats yet, so I discuss plumbing! Years ago, I ran across a book written by Dan Holohan of heatinghelp.com. The book is called *How to Teach Technicians*. Technicians are more visual and tactile than "regular" people. They want and need to touch things to understand them. I understand this rather well, as I am one. A little while ago I went looking for the book and found it was out of print, but the good news is that it has been updated and is now available again! The book walks you through the entire process of teaching, from knowing your audience, your material, and the room you'll be teaching in, to stories about the many ways teaching can get disrupted by things like dogs, crows, and very hot lightbulbs. Dan makes it clear how important humor and connecting with your audience are for getting good results.

I know his approach works. Some years ago, I was asked to give a talk on hot water at an American Water Works Association conference. I brought along a cut-out water heater as my main visual aid. All the other speakers seemed to be reading from their PowerPoint presentations, so when I came up with this water heater and other real things to pass around the room, people got excited. I noticed people in the audience calling their friends and telling them to "Get over here, you must see this presentation!"

That much excitement over hot water felt rather good. It gives me hope that if this excitement can happen with grownups, it can also happen with students who are in the process of choosing a career path.

I got to finish up the Parks class I mentioned by showing off what a plumber can do with copper. Liking cats, I made a copper "Cat in the Hat" using copper pipe and tube from 2″ to 1/4″ diameter. It demonstrates what you can do with silver solder and a little imagination. My message was that playing can be fun, and education can (and should) involve playing. Every day, I made a point of bringing in things that the students may not have run across and that could help with storytelling. One day I brought in a water heater from 1895 that still works and is more energy-efficient than most water heaters made today. Another day I brought in a bunch of old wrenches that, in concert, allow a plumber to work fearlessly on **any** pipe. I took in old water heater salesmans' samples, demonstrating how differently we used to think about hot water. We all had fun while learning! I don't know how learning and teaching can get much better.

 Look for the good in others. It may be hiding, but it's there.

What Isn't There

The fictional Sherlock Holmes was very good at noticing things. He could tell a lot just by looking at someone; people always offer clues about their background and circumstances if you know what to look for. One thing Sherlock taught me is to notice what isn't there. In one story, on a second visit to a crime scene, he noticed that something was missing. This, of course, led to the question of what was being hidden and why. This ultimately led to the bad guy being found

out. In this book, I'll be looking into some very different arenas to see what isn't there for us, and in some cases consider what we can do to fix it. People can be controlled by selecting what information they are given. We all usually try to make rational choices based on what we know. Some people have made fortunes by running toward things that most people are running away from. They know something others don't and have used it to profit. It may be that they look for patterns and see one repeating while others are just scared. Whatever it is, they see something that others don't. Sometimes what's "not there" can hurt us. I look at the schooling we have in the United States and wonder why serious financial education isn't offered. We should be getting this crucial training from the time we begin to learn about numbers, but we're left to figure it out for ourselves—or not. I imagine this is why so many Americans are in debt or have little to no savings. Way too many people are happy to borrow as much as they can and maintain credit card debt, but the financial overhead and monthly loss this brings makes me think that many us are simply modern-day serfs. (A serf is defined as: an agricultural laborer bound under the feudal system to work on his lord's estate.) It's essentially a form of enslavement. There is an ever-growing divide now between those who have lots of money and the rest of us. Recent numbers tell us that the top one percent of the U.S. population holds thirty-one percent of all wealth, while the bottom fifty percent holds one and a half percent. That's a pretty big difference, which I am confident has more to do with education than luck. Just as royalty is trained from childhood to think and act regally, being born with the silver spoon suggests a responsibility later in life to carry on and continue building that wealth. Financial education is just one form of education that isn't there for most of us, but money has such a huge effect on how people live their lives that it's past time we, both individually and as a society, prioritize the understanding of personal finance and monetary systems.

Here's another thing that many people don't see: similarities. We tend to focus on how others are different than we are. That might be useful information, but by ignoring the similarities we can easily create an "us versus them" mentality. We've done an exceptional job of it, as demonstrated by our politically divided country. This harms us individually and weakens us as a country. If we looked for ways in which we're alike, we'd more easily see the common ground and ways of working together. It's easy to see only our differences: rich vs. poor, black vs. white vs. brown, educated vs. not, skinny vs. big, religion vs. religion. But when we look at our similarities, the differences become far smaller and less important. And we have so many similarities! Another blind spot we seem to have is our health. Doctors are often treated like gods, whose dictates may not be questioned or debated, yet Western medicine basically just treats symptoms rather than getting to the root causes of disease. Western medicine is wonderful for things like broken bones and cuts, but seems lost when dealing with more complex problems like cancer or mental troubles. Compare it to the ancient science of Siddha-Veda, which looks not only at problems of the physical body but also at psychological and spiritual challenges. Siddha-Veda looks to heal the body, mind, and spirit. We've long known of the mind-body connection, but modern medicine mostly ignores it. Western medicine needs to look around at other healing modalities and learn from them, or risk being left behind, because it does not offer many deep or long-term health benefits.

Next, I'd like to address the concept of community. Community no longer exists for most of us in the meaningful ways we've historically enjoyed and benefited from. Humans are herd animals and always have been. Practically speaking, survival was more likely with a group of us together than going it alone. It was multi-generational, with elders teaching younger generations and the young ones entertaining and assisting their elders, each caring for the other in their own way. But that isn't how we live now. We're far more independent and isolated than ever before in human history. With relatively abundant and cheap energy, we can and do live independently of most others. With Covid, it became quite clear just how separated we've become. The incidence of mental distress spiked when we were cut off from our peers and social networks. Cohousing is an attempt to give us back a village, both physically and socially, and it works, but so far only thousands of people are getting the benefits of this, not billions. A meaningful community doesn't exist for many of us now, yet it's needed now more than ever. So many problems would disappear if we brought back strong communities. Right now, it just isn't there.

Lastly, I'd like to bring up the idea of "investing in yourself." We are taught to invest in things like the stock market, bonds, real estate, mutual funds, and such, but investing in yourself isn't even on the list of investments! Education is a form of self-investment. There are certainly lots of ways you can spend big bucks on schooling, but books, online info or training, and having mentors are very effective and usually far less expensive ways of getting the knowledge you want.

I like the example of tools as a form of self-investment. I enjoy using tools and I've had some of my tools now for over fifty years. I've used them on jobs I got paid for and wouldn't even have been able to do the work without those tools. Tools, when they get used, are a great investment! They can often pay for themselves in only one job and then get used on hundreds of jobs. If you only do ten jobs a year, that makes about a 1000 percent return on your investment. Try getting that with other legal investments! A good bank these days might pay you two percent.

So, the next time you're wondering how to invest for the best return, think about that investment nobody mentions: you. That just could be where the best returns will come from, but it's not really on the list of what people think of when they think of investments. I'm pretty sure there are many other things that "aren't there" for us. My point in writing this all down is to add another perspective, so we can begin to see what isn't there, and then act to make it better. Imagine the changes to your life if you were the king of money, saw the good in everyone, stayed in great health, had a loving community around you, and were always becoming even more capable. Imagine that!

 We create our own realities, by listening to only what we want to hear.

Just for One Day

I'd like to suggest a strange and simple experiment. It's a challenge and a test, and it just might bear sweet fruit. What if you took just one day in your life and paid attention only to what's  right and good in the world? Just one day! If you feel like it, keep a journal of some sort, make verbal notes on your smartphone, or whatever works for you.

We are so used to tempering what's right with what's wrong. Some folks live life as though nearly everything has risks or downsides. We often limit the positive out of fear that if we get used to it, it might go away and let us down.

I'm proposing living in the present and paying attention to all of the good in and around us. Sometimes all that good stuff is hard to see and feel, especially when our minds are living someplace in the future or the past. For example, if I look around me right now, I could focus on the overcast day or remember my cat who recently died way too young. Or I could go pick up that cat's sibling, who is still going strong, and pet him into purring and kneading the air. (Kneading the air is a cat's version of air guitar for humans. It's fun!) I could look outside and notice just how many types of birds are enjoying the seeds that I put out for them. I could notice that I'm comfortable in the house I built and that I'm in decent health. The present moment offers up much to be grateful for.

You usually don't need to look very hard to find good stuff. The problem is that we're often looking at what's amiss instead. The world will probably always have things that need fixing, but that doesn't mean we can't choose to have some stellar days! Even things that might be considered a burden, like the phone call from a talkative person that you know will take an hour of your time when you're trying to get stuff done. Think of it as a gift, teaching and helping you refine your ability to be patient and be a good listener—or a good boundary-setter. Paying attention to someone is a simple act, but it can be a game changer for them—particularly if they're feeling down and out. A few weeks ago, I was talking on the phone with a woman who just couldn't seem to get done what needed to get done. As she talked, I recognized the signs of her possibly being suicidal. She was a severe case of focusing only on what could go wrong. I couldn't sit with that, so I took two days and helped her get things done. Tears turned into laughter! Now that phase of her life is done and she's moving on to a brighter future. She just needed someone to be on her side for a bit. I get to know that I made a difference, so now I have one more positive outcome to think about while I'm only paying attention to what's right with the world!

Another little monster that does what it can to make us see only what's wrong is regret. Regrets haunt us and keep us from being fully present and aware of the world and its gifts to us. If you do your best, that old "if I had only known..." thought can't get a toehold. Things do change. New and better information comes along. But that's no reason to hammer yourself for past events if you did your best with what you knew. So, for this day of seeing what's right, put any regrets out of mind so they cannot cloud your vision.

The real hope and benefit of seeing what's right for a day is that it might just feel so good that you decide it's worth repeating the next day and the next, so that it becomes a rewarding way of life. There really isn't any risk other than having sore smile muscles! The world will most likely keep turning even if you take a day off from what could go wrong. So, as Bobby McFerrin sings, "Don't worry, be happy!"

"Knowledge is Power" —Francis Bacon

Francis Bacon was clearly an intelligent person. The quote above remains true at both large and small scales. Let's look at just one field: plumbing. If you learn a few things about plumbing, it can help you make things in your home safer, healthier, more comfortable, more satisfying, less expensive, and less time-consuming. Yay!

Here is an example: Think safety for a moment. What is unsafe about what you see in this picture? Three things jump out at me. First, notice that cap on the relief valve line? That's a good way to encourage the water heater to blow up! A thirty-gallon heater can explode with the force of two sticks of dynamite. This is a forty-gallon tank under a house. If it went kablooie, the house would be so damaged that it might not be worth rebuilding. Not to mention what happens to the people inside! Or how about that plumbers' tape acting as earthquake strapping? It's actually worse than nothing; it gives the illusion of being helpful, but in an earthquake, it can't hold the tank in place—a tank that weighs over 400 pounds when full of water. Not only that, but when the tank falls in a quake, the gas line will probably break, flooding the house with gas…causing an explosion and fire. Not good! Finally, look at the vent pipe. See how it's close to floor joists and not connected to a vent pipe that leads outside? Which is worse: the possibility of an earthquake causing a gas fire that kills the occupants, or killing the occupants with carbon monoxide or fire because of the bad vent pipe? (I'm happy to tell you that all these problems did get fixed—but without appropriate know-how, someone might look at that water heater and say how nice and efficient it is because of the insulation blanket!) With the right knowledge, dangerous conditions like the ones you see here won't get built in the first place.

Fortunately, you don't have to know everything yourself. It can be tricky, but you can find good people who do know what's needed to help you stay safe and on track. Very often, just knowing what questions to ask is powerful. Francis Bacon was clearly on the right track. He'd probably be pleased to know that his thoughts could help people in the future to safely live with equipment that didn't even exist in his time. He was good at capturing those universal truths!

 Know what your constant and unshakeable truths are.

It's so Obvious

I have a friend who sometimes seems rude to me. She's only interested in talking about herself and doesn't appear to have any interest or time to find out how I'm doing or what's up in my life. The friendship could feel pretty unbalanced at times. But then, I know she's been going through  some difficulties and has a hard enough time just trying to take care of the basics for her own well-being. I know she just tries to put on a happy face for everyone, because that's what we're supposed to do. I'm looking forward to her problems getting smaller so she can be comfortable being her true self again.

Many of us go to great lengths to hide how we're really doing inside. If we feel crummy physically or emotionally, we just suck it up. Even someone you know well can be doing badly, but you can't easily see it because they do such a good job of pretending to be just fine, thank you! So how are we supposed to know when a stranger who doesn't treat us very well is doing so because they're just feeling really crummy? How do we know that the poor treatment we get has nothing to do with us?

When you think of it like this, those seemingly unappreciative, uncooperative, mean-spirited, and rude people that you run into might be really nice folks on a different day when they're not in so much pain.

It's the training society gives us, and the common belief is that showing your problems and challenges to others is a sign of weakness. Many go to great lengths to put on a smile when they really feel like hiding or crying. Have you ever put on that smile? No wonder it's so easy to misunderstand someone else's true state when they hide it with a big smile or by being difficult.

It is useful to look at this because those little hurts we suffer sometimes hang on to us for a long time. They seem to add up too. That little slight you suffered as a kid, when the teacher ignored your raised hand and excited face in class, might still be haunting you a little, even now. You had the perfect answer! But if you knew that the teacher was having a bad day, and was just trying to get through it without having to go home sick, you probably wouldn't have felt so bad about your "mistreatment." We can't know everybody's circumstances, but it could be useful to imagine others have little (or big) demons they're battling, and then let their apparent insensitivity to you fall away.

Putting all these puzzle pieces together makes it quite clear that whatever it is, whatever is causing the discomfort or hurt, it's rarely about us. Time to smack my forehead, it's so obvious! And what's obvious really depends on where you see it from. It's all in the perspective, and this is a place where time is very generous to us. Time gives us the perspective we need to have the opportunity to see past events more clearly so that we can revisit those old hurts and then let 'em go. We can look at the unhappy ones and give them some compassion when they can't manage to be nice. That compassion is as much a gift for us as it is for them. We can just let that baggage go and feel a bit lighter. Sometimes the most obvious things are the hardest to see.

 Avoid acting from fear; fear begets more fear.

Honoring the Dead Men and the Mentors

What valuable lessons have you learned in life—and who did you learn them from? We often learn by being given the gifts of perspectives, techniques, or ideas from others. Sometimes that learning is direct, as when we have a mentor. Sometimes the learning is indirect, gained by carefully observing what has been done before. And sometimes we learn by noticing what not to do!

While useful lessons often come from those who are with us now, the greatest teachings are sometimes gifts from the "Dead Men." That's a term my friend Dan Holohan came up with. Dan has conversations regularly with the Dead Men through the books and articles they wrote. The discussions can

get pretty interesting as Dan tries to explain things like computers and cell phones to people who lived one or two hundred years ago! He works with and teaches about steam and other heating systems, and steam in particular can be quite mysterious for those who haven't studied it. The Dead Men taught Dan how to understand their work in a couple of ways. They wrote books that are spending time on the shelves of used bookstores, waiting for the right person to come along and get excited about them. Also, the Dead Men left their work. Often their work has layers of other people's uninformed work done to them, so it becomes necessary for the properly skilled and observant person to come along and see through all that mischief to the good bones of the original system. From there, the system can often be put back into good working order.

But it takes honoring the Dead Men to do it. You need to understand what they were thinking and what they had to work with, both in terms of tools and equipment. It even helps to know something about the times they lived in. If they were working in the Great Depression, you can be sure there were no frills in the original system. If they were working after the 1918 pandemic, you know they sized their systems to heat the uninsulated house on the coldest day of the year, with all the windows open and the wind blowing! Learning all this is a way of honoring them. You can also honor them by keeping their old systems going.

We are all going to be with the Dead Men someday. If you've built something really good, don't you hope to see it live on well past your time? Don't you hope others, many years from now, will look at what you've done, think highly of it, and want to keep it going, or use it as a stepping stone to accomplish even more? Imagine: With your work now, you can inspire people not yet born. You can encourage them to value creativity!

Then we have mentors. My mentors live on through me and certainly others, as well. They each had their quirks, as we all do. One of my mentors was Otello. His lens on life was different. He had a deep vein of creativity combined with a very good understanding of materials. This allowed him to "misuse" things in ways that worked. From making fake antique furniture that would fool even the experts to showing me how to unclog a big sewer line using a bundle of barbed wire and a school bus to pull that through the pipe. He lived and performed his work creatively. How about this…Have you ever had a paint brush stiffen with dried paint? Otello's way was a **lot** faster than soaking the brush: Hammer the bristles on an anvil, then put the brush to a wire wheel. In a few minutes, you get a supple and clean brush—though it might be about half an inch shorter. Simply, Otello taught me his version of creativity, which I still put to use almost daily.

An early mentor, Hap, made me think for myself and I'm still glad he did. When I was fourteen years old, he taught me about electricity. I had a string of Christmas lights to test and fix. I imagined that electricity was just electricity, and I should be able to test the lights individually to see which ones didn't light up. He watched. I touched a single bulb to 120 volts. It flashed and went out. I tried to get it to light again but it wouldn't. Hap explained that the lights all work together. Each one adds some resistance to the flow of electricity so that none of the bulbs take on too much and get burned out like the one I had just ruined. I finally got a picture in my mind and understood the difference between series and parallel wiring. Hap didn't make me feel bad for burning out that bulb. It was a powerful way to make me understand. Sometimes you need to break stuff to really understand its range and limits.

They may be crusty or harsh, but mentors love sharing what they've learned, especially with the right student. Some of my mentors were socially inept and difficult for most people to be around. But by showing an interest in their perspective and their knowledge, they became willing to take me under their wings and drop the abrasiveness (most of the time). I've mentored others and still do. Some of the people I taught are mentoring others now. I'm slowly handing over to them the job of making this world a better place.

What's the Worst that Could Happen?

I've been asking myself that question for a long time, and I find it helpful. As a young person, I was often told, "No, you can't do that!" and, "That's not how to do it!" But I have a tenacious streak. Grownups are supposed to know better, so I listened, but as I got more experience in the world, I  questioned the old beliefs, rules, and dogmas. Asking myself "what's the worst that could happen?" has helped me with sorting out which rules made sense and which ones really didn't apply. When asking the question, I often found that I was warned against doing anything other than the normal, accepted practice, just because something might go wrong. The world of plumbing offers up a good example. Plumbers have long prided themselves on running pipes straight and square. This may be pretty, but it isn't efficient! Pipes that run the shortest distance cost less in materials, and in a water supply system the goal is to waste less water and deliver hot water faster. Now, with flexible piping materials, it makes even more sense to take the shortest path. We no longer use threaded steel pipes like we used to do. That stuff needed to be run straight and square. So, in this case, only good things happen when you don't follow convention.

As a kid, I just loved climbing trees. We had lots of pine trees to climb, so I did. Bad things certainly could have happened. It might be a bit uncomfortable to fall fifty or more feet from your perch up in a tree. The worst that could happen might be to survive a fall like that and have a ruined body or mind! Even then I understood the risk, and learned to move slowly and carefully in the trees, keeping in mind what my next moves would be and what limbs I could trust. So, just knowing that bad things could happen didn't keep me from the experience of going where only the birds went, but it helped me to plan my actions, understand the properties of trees, and to fully respect gravity! Asking yourself "what's the worst that could happen" is an exercise in thinking something through and attempting to really understand it. It's a fact-based way of looking at things. This question has allowed me to make progress when others would have had me give up. A simple example of this is that it's long been known that gas fired water heaters make an annoying racket when sediment builds up at the bottom of the tank. The only real fix has been to replace the water heater. I developed a tool to vacuum out the sediment, quieting the heater. This is far less expensive than replacing it. I just had to step off the beaten path and ask a better question. The worst case would have been some time wasted building the tool. The unexpected better case was that I got to build lots of them for other plumbers and created a service business that supported me for many years!

"What's the worst that could happen?" is also a way of looking at things as if they were new, with no assumptions or emotional history cluttering up the decision-making process. It is not a "get out of jail free" card. If I felt like riding fast down a steep dirt road on my bicycle, asking "what's the worst that could happen?" could help me decide whether the thrill was worth the risk, but it wouldn't keep me from sliding off the road at that sharp turn and getting all scraped and banged up! That's called learning the hard way, and that's a whole other subject.

Fear also plays into this. Many of us are taught to be afraid of new or unusual things, or ways of doing them. We then use our imaginations to dream up things going horribly wrong, but things very seldom go as badly as our imaginations believe they can. Might it be better to use that powerful imagination to help you see ways of making things go right?

Pondering "what's the worst that could happen?" lets you see what really could go badly and take precautions to prevent that from happening. It actually increases your chances of success; those roadblocks are only there to challenge and strengthen your imagination so that you'll be better able to figure out ways around those blocks. This isn't magical thinking; it's a tool for better understanding how things can go so that you can plan better and be more successful in getting the things done that you want to do.

The Cat Meditation

I really need quiet time in my life. Without it, I've learned that I'm easily scattered, without focus, and miss obvious things. This morning, I laid down to get some of that quiet time, and Shadow the cat decided it was a good time to come help. He did so happily. He started kneading my shoulder and purring...a nice low, steady purr. So, instead of focusing on my own breath, I paid attention to his. I listened closely to his purring and let it push out nearly all other busy-ness from my mind. Cats purr when they're happy, or at least content, so I received the added gift of contented breathing instead of just moving air in and out! Shadow and I did this for some calming piece of time until he decided to get up and move on. His work was done.

Curiosity got to me. I've heard people talking about meditation for nearly forever, but there has never seemed to be a good definition of what it is. Is it a state of mind, something religious, something else, or all of the above? So, I looked it up and found basically that it's all of the above and probably a lot more, but one main point of it is to quiet your mind. I've long needed my quiet time to be able to let the puzzle pieces of life come together for me in a way that makes sense instead of having a jumble of bits to trip over. A common technique for finding this quietude is to pay close attention to your own breath. With skill and luck, you'll pay such close attention that the busy mind and random thoughts will leave you alone for a time. This way you can have the peace you need to allow the puzzle pieces of the world to settle, fit together, and make sense. It had never occurred to me that I could listen to another's breathing and get the benefits, but Shadow schooled me this morning.

Now, I'm wondering if the sound of crickets at night could do something similar. How about the breeze blowing through leaves? Heck, if you're in a city, maybe distant traffic could be just the thing. As long as we're not being inundated by the symbolism of words and the pressure of multiple interpretations they seem to bring, quiet time is within reach. Another thought occurred to this tactile person as I petted the purring cat. My hands inform and teach me things that are outside of the realm of words. My hands are quite content in the non-verbal world of cat petting. Might this be another path leading to the benefits of meditation or quiet time? Might putting your hands in a gentle stream, or simply feeling a warm breeze, give the focal point needed to immerse your entire self in quiet time?

A gift I get when experiencing quiet time is that "things fall in." By that, I mean when the constant background din of random thoughts is subdued, those things that are important and that I wished I could remember just come to me. It's as though my subconscious mind has kept track of what's important and is just waiting for an opportunity to say something, but my conscious chattering mind doesn't give it much opportunity. By paying attention to Shadow, or other non-symbolic input, my chattering inner dialogue gets to take a break and let my subconscious have a say. Who knew what gift a cat could give if I just paid attention? He's got a really nice purr!

Hot Water-Energy

How We Got into Hot Water

Water heaters generally work so well that they're the least thought-about equipment in homes. But when they misbehave, they can cause anything from a ruined family gathering to an explosion—or just the frustration of not being able to take a hot shower when you need one. It's a good idea to take time to understand water heaters, learn a little about their past, and guess at their future so that we can get the best performance and longest life from our water-heating systems.

In the beginning, there was cold water—so people didn't bathe much. They masked body odor with perfumes and oils, or just went around being smelly. As recently as 100 years ago, hot running water was available only to the wealthy. These days, in the United States, a personal supply of hot water is thought of as a necessity, right up there with food and shelter. Just try going without it!

Over time, people have heated water in many ways. A brief look at some of these methods can give perspective, and you will see how some of these older and now unused techniques could have application today.

From Stove to Storage Tank

When wood and coal were the prevalent fuels, water was usually heated in a pot over the fire or in a kettle over the cook stove. Some stoves had a reservoir lined with tin, copper, or porcelain; this would be filled with water for heating. Warming up enough water for a bath was a time-consuming ordeal, and much of Saturday was spent getting cleaned up for church on Sunday.

Later, when running water came indoors, a chamber or pipe loop called a "water back" (or water front) was installed in the firebox of the stove. Heated water would move by convection through this chamber to a storage tank. For reasons that can only be guessed at, these tanks were called range boilers, even though it was the oven that did the heating. Some of these old systems are still operating today. The oldest water-back/range boiler I've seen still in use dates back to the early 1920s. It's in an old homestead on a cattle ranch.

A variation of the stove/storage tank idea was the "scuttle-a-day" heater, which used coal. This was a small cast iron device. Short and squat, with a rounded top, it looked more like R2-D2 from *Star Wars* than a water heater. Hooked up to a storage tank in the same way as a water back, it used about one scuttle (bucket) of coal per day to keep the water hot. Using the scuttle-a-day eliminated the need to fire up the kitchen stove when hot water was needed. It saved fuel and avoided  turning the house into a sauna during hot weather. This heater had damper controls to adjust the rate of burning, but fully automatic water heating was yet to come.

Another interesting type of water heater was the side-arm. This heater was hooked up beside the tank and piped in, high and low. It usually had a gas burner placed underneath a copper coil. These were commonly "holstered" in a cast iron shell. Water would be heated in the coil, then convection would drive the heated water to the storage tank, just as it did in the water-back and scuttle-a-day coal burners.

Originally, side-arm water heaters simply had a gas valve that was operated by hand. The gas was lit with a match when you wanted a bath. Forgetting to shut if off when done with the bath "triggered" a potentially explosive situation. Later, automatic controls and safeties were developed that made the side-arm heaters easier to live with. One advantage of the side-arm heater was that if its storage tank rusted out, you could simply replace that one component. You'd transfer the burner and other pieces to your new tank, keeping costs down. Planned obsolescence had not yet become a way of life.

It's interesting to note that one of the most efficient water heaters (no longer available) was the Marathon gas-fired heater. It was an updated side-arm heater. One of the main reasons it was so efficient is that the burner was separated from the storage tank. Because there was no flue running up through the stored hot water, standby heat loss from the water heater was greatly reduced.

Hot Water in an Instant

Up until the 1890s, all types of water heaters both heated and stored the water. Kerosene, gasoline, and a variety of gasses have been used to heat water. (Some gasses, such as acetylene and producer gas, could even be made on site.) With the advent of high-energy liquid and gaseous fuels,

instantaneous water heating became
possible. These fuels were much easier
to regulate automatically than wood or
coal.

The bath heater was one of the first
instantaneous types. I find one variety
particularly interesting. Once a pilot
was lit, turning on the water would also
turn on the gas burner. Water flowed
up through a pipe to a sprinkler inside
the top of the unit. As water sprayed
out through the combustion gasses,
it collected heat (and combustion
byproducts). From there, the water
cascaded over metal that was being
heated by the flame, collecting more heat. The water then traveled
around to a spigot and into the tub.

Ad copy in the 1906 Sweet's Catalog boasted that this method
utilized "ninety-two units of heat out of a possible 100, a feat never
before accomplished in heater construction."

This water heater was extremely efficient, though it did result in
slightly tainted bath water. Perhaps the somewhat acidic water cleaned
better! Today, the most efficient furnaces and boilers also cool down
the flue gasses enough so that they condense and give up even more
heat to the water.

As the Century Turned

At present, only three manufacturers, AO Smith, Bradford White, and
Rheem produce most of the water heaters in the United States. In the
early 1900s, there were over 150 manufacturers. Back then, many types
of water heaters competed for customer dollars. The two major types of
water heater available were "automatic instantaneous" and "automatic

storage" heaters. You already know which type prevailed. Automatic storage water heaters now make up about ninety-eight percent of all heaters sold.

This may have to do with how people bathe. For many reasons, precise temperature control has always been difficult with instantaneous water heaters (also known as tankless). That didn't matter when filling a tub, which is what almost everybody used to do. As toes tested the water, hot or cold was added until the bather was satisfied. When the "rain bath" or shower became more common, if the water temperature fluctuated during the shower, it was noticed …and not much appreciated. Tank-type heaters seemed to gain in popularity around this time because they could produce very steady water temperatures.

Galvanized steel tanks were common, but longer-lasting copper, bronze, and Monel (a copper-nickel mix) were also available. Performance improved dramatically when insulation was added to the tank—surprise! (What seems obvious to us now was innovative back then.) Like the side-arm water heater, some of the early tank-type heaters were designed so that you could replace just the tank and reuse the rest of the components, including the insulation.

In the past, people didn't keep water hot all the time just waiting for it to be used. They fired up the heater when they planned on using hot water. Because tankless water heaters could produce hot water as soon as the pilot was lit, tank-type water-heater makers were probably at a competitive disadvantage. Inventors came up with some innovative ways of getting hot water from a tank within a few minutes after heating had begun.

One method placed a coil of pipe in the combustion chamber. Water was fed into the coil from the bottom of the water heater. A tube ran from the coil up the flue and connected to the hot outlet pipe. Water was heated in the coil almost immediately; it could either be used right then or sent to storage.

Another method wrapped a jacket about an inch away from and completely around the flue, surrounding it inside the tank. This jacket was open both top and bottom, creating a rising current of heated water. As with the previous method, hot water was almost instantly available for use, although in a limited quantity.

These tank-type water heaters still took as long as ever to heat their entire contents, but they could provide a small amount of hot water quickly for chores. That meant the water heater could be turned on briefly and then kept off most of the time, greatly cutting heat losses from the tank when it wasn't being used.

Early Solar Thermal

Solar water heating (also known as "solar thermal") started catching on around the late 1800s. Originally there were batch heaters, now called internal collector and storage (ICS) units. These heaters had one or more tanks placed behind glass in an enclosed box. They were very simple, with no moving parts and little risk of freeze damage. Their main drawback was substantial overnight heat loss.

Thermosyphon systems were an improvement. This method placed the tank above the collector and used natural thermal convection to move heated water into the tank (just like the side-arm heater). One manufacturer was Day and Night, so called because their heaters provided hot water both day and night. Their insulated tanks kept stored water hot after the sun went down, and that was a solar first.

The company suffered when unusually cold weather caused freeze damage to many of their collectors. Their remedy was to fill the collector with alcohol and water, and install a heat exchanger between the tank and the collector. This was a non-toxic, freeze-proof solution to cold weather. I personally feel this was one of the most elegantly simple and efficient solar water-heating systems ever devised.

A second problem occurred as solar tanks aged and began to leak. A major cause of leaks then, as now, was using different metals together in water. When metals are mixed this way, one of them always corrodes to protect the other. One metal turns bodyguard to the more "noble" metal, and it sacrifices itself. Thus, steel rusts away to protect copper. When these metals were used together, plumbing corroded and holes developed. Water leaked out and caused havoc. Today, plastic-lined steel nipples and dielectric unions can be used effectively to separate the metals and prevent this problem.

There was yet another common problem. Solar thermal tanks were usually installed in attics, up under the peak, so that thermosyphoning with the roof-mounted solar collectors could work. When tanks leaked, this created a major headache. Even if they had not been packed in boxes with cork bits all around, access to attic tanks was difficult. Replacement would have been a nightmare, and it probably was seldom attempted. Instead, tanks or their plumbing failed, houses flooded, and solar thermal developed a black eye. If only the owners had been informed about galvanic corrosion and the use of sacrificial anodes to protect their tanks! Just as steel rusts to protect copper, sacrificial anodes corrode away to protect steel and other metals used in plumbing.

At this time, gas was becoming more widely available, and its price was very attractive. Utility companies even got into the business of selling water heaters (free bath towels included) to build demand for their product. Solar thermal was not able to compete against low gas prices or the freedom from system maintenance that abundant utility energy offered. Solar water heating slowly disappeared.

Tank Evolution

Meanwhile, tank-type electric and gas water heaters took over the lion's share of the market. Tank-building technology was changing, and as energy prices started going up, attempts were made to make tanks more efficient.

One such tank was the "U" tube water heater. It's enlightening to compare it to present-day water heaters. Modern gas water heaters have a flue, which usually consists of a three- to four-inch-diameter pipe running from the combustion chamber below the tank up through the center of the tank. It also acts as a chimney when the burner is off, so warmed air is constantly flowing up and out through it. This is all lost heat.

In the "U" tube heater, the flue ran up inside the tank until it got near the top. Then it made a 180-degree turn and headed back down. It exited near the bottom and connected to an external vent pipe. This inverted U created a heat trap. It would vent only when the burner fired, and so lost much less heat. Also, since the U doubled the surface area of the pipe inside the tank, more heat was captured by the water. It was very efficient. Unfortunately, the manufacturers felt the need to compete based mostly on price; the "U" tube heater wasn't the cheapest to make, so it fell by the wayside. Another change in manufacturing was the advent of glass tank lining. This glass coating is similar to ceramic glazing. Baked onto the inside of a steel tank, it provides a very good defense against rusting. Because a perfect process for glass-lining tanks has yet to be developed, sacrificial anode rods are used to protect the steel at any imperfections in the lining.

This system worked so well that manufacturers eventually stopped making tanks of expensive metals such as copper and Monel. Instead, their better tanks were made of extra-heavy steel lined with a double coating of glass. With such good protection and thick steel, a tank could last decades after its anode was used up. In fact, I recently ran across a forty-two-year-old water heater that is still in good condition.

As the business of making and selling water heaters grew ever more competitive, manufacturers found ways to cut costs. As tanks were made of thinner steel and double-glass lining was no longer offered, tank quality began to deteriorate. Metal drains were replaced with plastic.

Experience has shown us that modern tanks are more delicate than their predecessors, but with maintenance their service lives can still be greatly extended. The average life of tank-type water heaters is nine to twelve years, but with periodic maintenance I've gotten fifty years from them! More expensive tanks today may have a second anode, or they may have a plastic lining or be made entirely of plastic to prevent corrosion. Still, the lower-priced glass-lined tanks make up the vast majority of tanks in service and sold today.

Safety and Energy Upgrades

There have been ongoing efforts to make water heaters safer. The results have been so successful that, at one point, it was suggested that we didn't need to install relief valves anymore because tanks had quit blowing up! Tanks do explode less often today, precisely because relief valves do get installed and because water heaters now have better controls. But they can still explode, and we absolutely do still need relief (T&P) valves!

Manufacturers have also been fine-tuning water heaters for better energy performance to meet stringent federal energy codes. This has pros and cons. Yes, plastic drain valves lose less heat than brass ones, but very often they simply don't work. Yes, some small amount of heat is lost through the anode's exposed hex head, but proposals to insulate and cover the hex head may do more damage than good; unless access to the anode remains, anode replacement and water heater maintenance would become much more difficult.

Energy-efficiency of hot water systems is likely to get even more attention in the future. Once the water heaters themselves have been tweaked for every BTU of performance, it will make sense to zero in on the antiquated pipe distribution systems through which many of those BTUs are lost. Other areas ripe for improvement include heat recovery and reducing consumption of hot water.

▲▲▲

You can see that by better understanding the history and the likely future of your otherwise out-of-sight-out-of-mind water heater, you can maximize your chances of staying happy and healthy. It's the best way to stay in hot water!

Water and Energy: Fixing the Leaks

Water requires a great deal of energy. In California, for example, extracting, treating, moving, heating, and disposing of it account for about thirty percent of the state's total energy usage. That's a lot! What can we do to reduce water and energy waste for ourselves?

Houses need replumbing sometimes and this is a great opportunity to save water and energy…and get better performance from the system. By the way, installing an efficient plumbing system can cost less than putting in an inefficient system! Manifold and demand systems are two approaches to look at. Simply installing low-flow fixtures can backfire if hooked up to an inefficient system. It will slow flow rates in the lines and cause longer waits for hot water at the shower and elsewhere.

Manifold plumbing, to put it simply, means running an individual small line to each fixture. If the fixtures are close together, as is common in older homes, this could be a great way to save water and energy and get hot water much faster. Also, it could mean running small (like 3/8″) tubing to the fixtures, which is much easier than running larger pipe. Demand controlled systems use the typical main and branch plumbing, but add a pump to push the cooled water out of the hot line into the cold or a dedicated return, so when you turn on a tap, you get hot water quickly with far less waste. They are great for retrofits where the plumbing system is basically sound, but inefficient.

The simple act of heating water seems to divide us into different camps. Tank-type heaters versus tankless. This is a question where all the circumstances around what heater is used need to be considered. Will the owner maintain the equipment? How hard is the water? Tankless heaters don't like hard water. What sort of hot water service is needed? A one-size-fits-all approach really doesn't fit here!

And then there is the 120-degree water vs. 140-degree question... or named differently, Legionnaires' disease vs. scalding. The plumbing community still doesn't fully agree on how to make this decision. There are a variety of mixing or tempering valves which can help, but hard water or incorrect sizing will play havoc on them. If there are any very old, young, or immune compromised people in the house, it makes sense to store the water hotter and then mix it down to a safe temperature. Otherwise, I like to keep water around 130 degrees and just be careful when using it. Having the heater hooked up to efficient plumbing will go a long way towards making the water better/safer for use, as well. If the piping is sized right, water will travel down the line at a rate of at least one foot per second. This will scrub the lines, helping prevent slime and bacteria from growing in the pipes. Staying healthy is a nice side benefit of efficient plumbing!

Still, whatever the equipment or its usage, opportunities likely exist, depending on building shape and orientation for energy savings via heat recovery and/or solar heating. Shower drain heat recovery is one great way to plug an energy leak. It can capture sixty percent of the energy that would have gone down the drain. Efficient fixtures on small lines are another approach. Running hot water only to places that actually need it is another. Many dishwashers can heat their own water, so a hot supply isn't needed. Clothes may not need to be cleaned in hot water, as modern detergents can do the job. Certainly, other opportunities will show up if we look for them.

Maintenance can greatly extend equipment life. I've gotten fifty years from tank-type water heaters with simple maintenance, yet we're told to worry if the heater is over ten. A life-cycle cost approach can be used to bring order when thinking about water heating choices. When all costs over time are taken into account, it becomes easy to see what equipment really costs less and which approach saves the most energy and water. Then you can factor in the savings in waiting times, headaches when equipment fails on holidays, and reduced risk of flooding and property damage.

On another topic, outdoor water usage may be controlled with thoughtful yard design, grey water, and rainwater catchment. Houses often use far more water outdoors than inside. People think pools use a lot of water, but then don't think about their lawns!

Looking at our overall water usage, compared to other countries, there is just a little room for improvement. Around the world, the most water efficient people are in Africa, using as little as 392 cubic feet of water per person per year. In America, we use from 36,600 to 189,740 cubic feet per year! That's up to 484 times as much. We're amongst the least water efficient in the world. I imagine we can do a bit better. The Western U.S. is looking at another drought, so we have no choice but to do better, and quickly. I've found that with energy efficiency, it's not all that hard to get by comfortably on twenty percent of the power most people use. I imagine we can do something similar with water if we step away from old habits and get creative.

I know I've wandered all over the world with these ideas, but hopefully have given you some ideas and things to look into to get the benefits of saving water and energy for yourself.

Energy Efficiency...How Far Can it Go?

I'm a big fan of making things efficient. It's a powerful tool for improving one's life, yet it seems to be poorly understood. It's common for people to take some basic energy efficiency measures, then think, "I've already done that...nothing more to do."

For example, thinking about electricity usage for a bit, if we take measures that save us twenty-five percent on our bill, that feels quite nice, and then we turn our attention elsewhere. But we can do far better. I have a friend who recently cut his electricity usage by sixty percent just by looking at lighting and refrigeration. But he's not stopping there; now he's looking at other ways to cut consumption.

Have you looked at your electricity bill recently? A large percentage of the bill is for stuff you don't directly benefit from, like surcharges and taxes for some program you probably don't qualify for. Even if you do not use any electricity, just being hooked up has a cost. I'll posit that it's possible to get a ninety percent reduction in electricity usage—all energy usage, for that matter—but it's not easy. It requires some different thinking, like considering money spent on upgrades as an investment rather than focusing on the first cost. Looked at this way, you can figure out how this investment compares to others and also compare the safety of these investments.

"Life cycle cost" is another way of thinking about energy-efficiency investments. This approach compares ALL costs over time and allows you to "race" one technology against another to see which performs better in the long term. Sometimes the most energy-efficient equipment costs more than the less efficient stuff because of increased maintenance costs for certain equipment. Think of very efficient condensing water heaters or boilers for a minute. They do indeed save energy, but must have yearly maintenance. The cost of that maintenance can eat up any savings from using less energy. Who knew?

But imagine what happens when you do achieve such a large reduction in your energy usage. Eliminating the remaining ten percent becomes pretty simple by generating the power yourself. This allows you to consider disconnecting from the grid and getting rid of all those surcharges. It does mean you need to be responsible for your own home electrical system, which usually means spending a few minutes each week checking on things.

So, are you ready to drastically reduce your energy consumption? Let's start with your electricity bills. Gather up a year's worth, and notice how your electricity consumption goes up and down from season to season. If you look at summer bills, there should be little or no heating cost. In winter, your AC unit probably isn't running. The shoulder seasons (spring and fall), when heating and cooling are not used much, are the best timeframe for seeing just what your lowest or standby load is. That's the energy you use when nearly everything that can be turned off is off. An ideal way to get this number would be to see how much power your home used while you were away on vacation. I've looked at the standby load in my house, and it's under 15 watts. In many homes, it's over 300 watts! This load often comes from electronics that don't get turned off, like remote-controlled TVs or ground-fault outlets. The cost of those 300 watts gives you little in return, and it's one of the best places to look when starting to trim your electricity usage.

I've found that a Kill-O-Watt meter is a great investment (about $28). It lets you accurately measure energy usage for your appliances, so that you'll know which are really using up power. It's commonly available at big box hardware stores. To use it, you just plug it into an outlet and plug the appliance to be measured into the meter. Measure your TV's electricity consumption when it's turned on, and also when it's off. You may find that it uses more energy during the hours when it's turned off than when you're watching TV! Even though the power draw is less when it's off, if you watch two hours a day, that power it sips for twenty-two hours can add up to much more than the power it used for those two hours when you watched it. Now, if you simply put your TV on a power strip, you can eliminate that waste by turning the power strip off when you're not watching.

The concept is simple: Measure your usage and keep track of where power is going. Then you can look at good alternatives, such as more efficient equipment, power strips, eliminating unnecessary electric draws, and even supplementing with solar-electric panels. For example, using a simple solar-thermal preheat for your electric water heater can have a big impact on your bill. For a **lot** more information about this concept, I suggest visiting www.thousandhomechallenge.com, to learn about the Thousand-Home Challenge. Here, you'll find case studies on how people made their homes highly efficient—often using a lot of creativity, which can be very inexpensive! You'll even see that my home was the thirteenth one to meet the challenge.

So far, I've just been talking about electricity. But the concept of efficiency works in many other areas: water, gas, trash, transportation, home size, and maybe even money! With any of these, you would first measure to learn where the big consumers are. Then you can look at ways of dealing with them. Here's a quick example of how to use water more efficiently. After measuring your current usage, let's say you find that you use twice as much water for irrigation as you use indoors. Maybe putting in a rainwater catchment system would be a good thing; it could conceivably cut water needs for irrigation down to nearly nothing. For transportation, you could add extra solar-electric panels to your roof and use them to power an electric car. Just a little creativity can go a long way when it's driving efficiency!

 Live below your means so that money worries can fade.

Now You're Cooking with Gas!

In July of 2019, Berkeley, California, banned future gas hookups in new construction. It's been causing quite the uproar. It seems there are roughly fifty other jurisdictions considering a similar move. I'm in an interesting position; I'm a member of a decarbonization group, which is

A two "burner" induction cooktop

essentially against burning fossil fuels (for a number of reasons: health and safety, climate change, and saving money), and I'm a member of an online community of technicians who do heating/cooling of all sorts—and life without burning gas or oil would be a major shift for them. The views of the two groups are rather different; or perhaps I should say they are based on different sets of facts.

How did gas come to be so ubiquitous in homes and commercial buildings? In the 1930s, the natural gas industry made a big marketing push for gas-powered stoves. They created the phrase "Now you're cooking with gas," meaning "you're on the right track."

It was heard on popular radio shows and worked its way into common parlance. Perhaps it's time to create a new phrase to say, "You're doing fabulously!"

For decades, gas has been sold to us on the premise that it was clean. It has been considered clean compared to coal, and if you look only at emissions from combustion, that's true. But if you also consider gas leakage, the story is different. There are leaks where gas is generated, in the distribution system, and where it's being used. Looking only at the distribution system, it's generally agreed that, on average, four percent of what goes into the system leaks out before making it to the end users. Natural gas is basically methane, which is a potent greenhouse gas. Depending on the source, it's thought to be twenty-five to eighty times more potent than carbon dioxide, meaning it is that much more effective at trapping heat on our planet. So, that four percent leakage makes gas a dirtier fuel than coal. Who'da thunk?! Gas utilities have not kept up with the maintenance of their aging infrastructure, so it leaks. A couple of big, unhappy examples of this are from San Bruno, California and Aliso Canyon, near Los Angeles. For more information, search online for "Fires Starting With Flammable Gas Fact Sheet."

Did you know that natural gas and propane give us:

- 168 civilian deaths per year
- 1,029 civilian injuries per year
- $644 million per year in direct property damage

Perhaps Berkeley is different in that there just might be some residual memory of the San Francisco earthquake and fire of 1906. Leaking gas was the catalyst for the fires, which destroyed about 500 city blocks with 28,000 buildings, so perhaps the present inhabitants are more sensitive to the dangers of gas than populations in other areas.

Now let's talk about the health effects of burning gas in our homes. Search online for "Cooking with Gas Can Harm Children" and you'll find a report on what the effects are. Quoting from the report:

The analysis showed that children living in a home with a gas cooking stove have a forty-two percent increased risk of current asthma (ninety-five percent confidence interval [CI] 1.23, 1.64), and a twenty-four percent increased lifetime risk of asthma (CI 1.04, 1.47).

Lawrence Berkeley National Labs has done a bunch of research on the pollution caused by gas cooking. Apparently, it's common for indoor levels of nitrous oxide and other pollutants to reach levels that would require abatement actions if they were outside. Nobody would knowingly subject their children (or themselves) to this. Might it be time to consider induction cooking? (Let's not forget to investigate any electromagnetic pollution these cookers may cause!)

There is another concept floating around out there called bio-gas, also known as renewable gas and similar names. Landfills, cattle ranches, and sewer plants all produce methane, which normally just escapes into the atmosphere. Capturing that gas and putting it to work could do plenty of good. It could fuel fleets and/or be used to generate electricity. As it wouldn't need to go into a leaky distribution system, the leakage problems would go away, and the gas could go from being a driver of climate change to being a useful energy source. Monterey County in California has a landfill in Marina that has been capturing methane successfully for years. It clearly works!

I'm a proponent of energy-efficiency. With some work, buildings can be made sixty to eighty percent more energy-efficient. This isn't pie-in-the-sky imagining, but rather an intelligent use of technologies that we all have access to, along with plentiful helpings of elbow grease. Now, let's start by making buildings and their systems more energy-efficient. With that done, we can switch from gas-fired furnaces and water heaters to electric heat pumps, which will only need to sip electricity. This way, the power grid won't be stressed with increased demand. And, by the way, those energy-efficiency measures can pay for themselves at roughly a twenty-five percent yearly return. That's *far* better than almost any traditional investment that isn't breaking some law.

Looking ahead, I can see that we'll need to make most existing buildings far more energy-efficient and healthier to live in. We may also want to prepare for the inevitable change away from gasoline-powered to electric vehicles. Making our buildings more energy-efficient, and even capable of being self-powered (or off-grid), while providing for electric-vehicle charging would drive an entire industry. Making our buildings safer and healthier would also improve quality of life while cutting health costs.

Here is where we can utilize those smart tradespeople who want to do the best for their clients. They already have a good grasp of the essential concepts of building science and can put them to use in the massive undertaking of making our world safer, healthier, and more prosperous than ever, while keeping an eye on the long-term benefits to all of life. Now *that's* "cooking with gas!"

How Much Power Do We Really Need?

I built my home to be as energy-efficient as I could. I did this because I planned to live off-grid and needed to generate my own power. The less power I needed, the smaller, less expensive, and easier to manage my "power plant" could be. Back when I was designing this system, photovoltaic panels were not inexpensive, so I was motivated to be very efficient—and I wanted to see just how far I could push things. Bringing

utility power to my place in the sticks would probably have cost about $75,000 and given me monthly utility bills to boot, so I really didn't want to go in that direction. I needed to ponder some questions, which are largely the same whether it's for a planned off-grid home or an existing home tied to the grid:

1. How will every bit of power be used?

2. Which systems and appliances are very efficient?

3. What loads can be shed?

4. Where are the phantom loads?

Before I get to my list, I'd like to point out that being really energy efficient doesn't have to hurt or be a struggle. There is no need to cramp your lifestyle to do this. It's not about sacrifice, or freezing in the dark, or wearing two sweaters and a jacket. It's really about having the necessary information and putting it to good use! So here we go.

1. How will every bit of power be used? The process for figuring out loads in an existing home is different than doing this for a not-yet-built home, but there are similarities. With an existing home, you can measure actual usage over time and don't need to guess at how many hours a day, things might be used.

A simple way to estimate how much power is needed by an existing home is to use a form (readily available online) that names the various loads and how many hours a day they will probably be used. But that's just a rough estimate. I've found that name-tag data (the efficiency numbers on the product's label) doesn't reflect actual power consumption most of the time either. But checking consumption with a "Kill-a-Watt" meter, or possibly an ammeter, gives a good idea of actual consumption. This is my preferred method, as it gives the information I need to make things efficient and to size equipment for making my own power.

Measuring is pretty hard to do if the house isn't built yet or you don't already own the appliances and fixtures, so you get to make educated guesses. This can be done by measuring how long you use your current appliances and then comparing name-tag data of your current and future appliances to get a rough idea of what percentage reduction you can expect from a new, more efficient appliance. Then you can measure the actual energy use of the current appliance and apply that percent reduction to come up with a daily or weekly anticipated energy use. This approach is particularly important if you plan on being off-grid or powering your house when the grid goes down. You need to be able to store enough power to tide you over.

2. Which systems and appliances are very efficient? The electrical code when I built my house allowed a two percent energy loss in the wiring. This is where the electricity simply turns to heat along the length of the wire. I didn't want to build that waste in, so in some places I upgraded the wire by one size to cut that potential loss. For example, long ago I had a desktop computer, but laptops are much more energy-efficient than desktops, and more portable when needed, so I switched to a laptop.

Also, what uses energy efficiently changes with time. I built the house to use compact fluorescent lights, because fluorescent lighting is much more efficient than incandescent. How old hat that seems now! This was before LEDs came into their own. Now I'm replacing my fluorescent lights with LEDs because they use less power, hold up better, and are less toxic in disposal.

3. What loads can be shed? Shedding loads means eliminating power consumption around the home. The first thing I did was to eliminate the electrical load of refrigeration by going to a gas fridge. That was a learning experience! It turns out that a gas fridge is so inefficient that it greatly increased not only my propane use, but also the overall energy use of the home. I switched to efficient electric refrigeration. This is a chest-style freezer, modified to act as a fridge. Starting with a chest-style unit is efficient, because even if the seals don't work too well, cold air cannot fall out of the fridge or freezer because the seals are all up on top of the unit. Also, it's better insulated. Modifying a freezer to use

as a fridge is done simply by adding an external thermostat that the "freezer" plugs into. That wound up being much better (although I now have a fridge humming away, where before I had a silent gas unit—but it's worth the energy savings).

Another thing I did to shed loads was to design my new home for daylighting (using the sun to light interior spaces) as much as possible. In addition to careful window placement, this involved making openings in interior walls to let daylight through, and painting ceilings bright white to reflect light better. A half-moon even lights the house adequately for getting around at night!

The energy used to power electric lighting is a small load in itself, but because I was building off-grid, I'd need an inverter to convert DC (from the photovoltaic solar panels) to AC power. That inverter would have to "wake up" for lights or other small loads, and it draws a fair amount of power just to be awake, even if it's powering only a fifteen-watt light. I sidestepped this by using twenty-four-volt DC lighting that runs directly off the batteries. An additional benefit is that if the main inverter is down for any reason, I still have lights. Modifying plug-in lamps to run on twenty-four volts is pretty easy.

Another trick was with the ground-fault (GFCI) outlets. I learned that GFCI outlets draw about one watt apiece, all the time. GFCI breakers draw about 1/4 watt. I needed to install sixteen GFCI-protected outlets, so I did this on three circuits using GFCI breakers which together draw only 3/4 of a watt instead of the sixteen watts that sixteen GFCI outlets would have drawn. The inverter comes out of sleep mode with a fifteen-watt draw. When "awake," the unit itself draws fifty-five watts. That's why it was important to design the house to use less than fifteen watts when sitting idle. By contrast, many grid-tied homes have a 300-watt draw all the time. This can be a combination of any and all sorts of electronics that don't get turned off, like GFCI outlets, TVs with remotes, cable boxes, and so on. That's a load worth shedding!

4. Where are the phantom loads? Phantom loads are power draws that occur much or all of the time, yet don't really contribute to living better in the house. TVs with remotes are a perfect example; they need to be awake and ready to see the remote signal when you press a button. This simple convenience means that most TVs use more power during the time when they're not being watched than when they are.

I've already described a few ways to eliminate phantom loads from GFCI outlets and lighting, but another effective way to cut phantom loads with things that plug in is simply to plug the electricity-guzzling appliances into power strips. Do make sure to use power strips that don't have electronics or little lights, or they create phantom loads of their own. I know it may seem crazy to pay attention to tiny draws of a watt or less, but they add up. Not catching these small losses would be like designing a plumbing system with a bunch of little drips. You just don't want to do that! Combining these measures allowed me to use only 960 watts of photovoltaic panels, which is less than half the size of a normal "small" system. That saved me a lot of money!

One more thing to consider: design and build your system so it's simple. "Simple" makes things easier to build—and troubleshoot if needed. Simple is durable. Simple costs less. Simple means you are less likely to have to rely on a technician to keep it running. You can probably tell I like simplicity!

In addition to the many benefits of energy efficiency, I want to make a plug for being off the grid: *when grid power is out around here (which happens more and more, as the regional utility resorts to planned power outages during fire season), it has no effect at my house.* It's handy to be in control of your power.

After all was done, it turns out that my place uses about one tenth of the energy per square foot of what the average home does and I think it's at least as comfortable. So, to answer the title question, we don't need nearly as much power as we might think if we take steps to keep things efficient through design and thoughtful use.

Take care of others and you will always be taken care of
somehow.

How to Look at a Water Heater

For years, I've been teaching classes
on how to understand the life and
death of water heaters. I do this
by catching water heaters on their
way to the dump, then taking them
apart. Sometimes fun tools like the
Sawzall or a really big pipe wrench
get used. It's instructive to actually
see what happens to water heaters
over time in different conditions.
You can even tell how much (or
how little) knowledge the people
had who came into contact with
the water heater during its lifetime.
The information here can help you
to become one of those people who
knows how to give their water
heater a long, safe life!

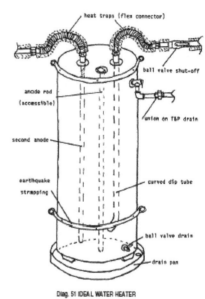

Diag. 51 IDEAL WATER HEATER

*Here is an ideal water heater. It's a basic
tank with no energy affiliation.*

The following is a brief overview of how to look at a water heater.
For a water heater that's still in service, these steps will tell you if it's
worth maintaining and how safe it is or isn't.

Determine the Water Heater's Age

We start by figuring out how old the water heater is, because you would
expect different issues from a four-year-old heater than from a forty-
year-old one!

This is done by looking for date codes on the heater itself, or on the relief valve or the controls. Sometimes there is even a date code on the dip tube, located inside the tank. A81 means January of 1981, B81 would be February, and so on. 181 also would mean January of 1981. 281 would be February. 8101 would be the first week of 1981, while 8152 would be the last week of 1981. Bradford White has their own code, which is available on their website: bradfordwhite.com.

Look at the Water Heater for Clues About Drafting

If it's a fuel-fired water heater, looking for signs of how well it's drafting can tell you how well the heater "breathes" and how safe it is—or not. If you see evidence of backdrafting, that means carbon monoxide may be getting into the living space. Not good! Looking at the photo to the right, notice the flue, curved sheet metal draft hood, and vent pipe in the center. On either side of this are the pipe nipples carrying cold water in and hot water out of the tank. Along with the relief valve towards the right.

top of gas water heater

hot combustion chamber showing discoloration

Do you see any of these things when looking at your water heater?

Corrosion on the flue side of the pipe nipple (a clear indicator of backdrafting). Nearly all tanks have a hot and a cold pipe nipple on top of the tank.

Melted insulation at the pipe nipples. This indicates hot fumes spilling out/backdrafting.

A ring of rust or discoloration on top of the water heater (acidic condensation may drip down onto the heater, causing a ring of rust; it's a sign of poor draft).

Discoloration or soot around the combustion chamber door (this is where flames or hot gasses leap out of the combustion chamber, suggesting a blocked flue or other problem).

Look in the Combustion Chamber

Do you see any evidence of leakage in the combustion chamber or flue? This matters because there is no point in working on a tank that has already failed. It's also a first clue about the condition of the anode inside the tank. If you find heavy or wet rust, the tank has leaked and is not worth fixing.

Remove the Anode and Assess Its Condition

Removing anodes can be challenging, and having good tools really matters. For this job, the best tool is a torque multiplier. This is a tool that pros use; it helps prevent unnecessary strain on the person doing the work. Next best (and less expensive) is a breaker bar that you tap with a mallet to loosen the anode.

torque multiplier with 12-point socket and 1/2" drive

Two anodes. On the left is the hex head type, and the other is the hot outlet combined with anode.

Most residential anodes need a 1-1/16″ socket. Get the six-point style as it will grab the anode better. Now after turning water off and relieving pressure, you can use that socket, breaker bar, and mallet to loosen the anode and get it turning. If the anode in your heater is combined with the hot outlet pipe, you can simply use a large (18″ or bigger) pipe wrench to unscrew it.

Once the anode is out...

Is the metal on the core wire depleted? (This lets you know how much life the anode has left.)

Is the anode magnesium or aluminum? (Aluminum is soft and easy to bend. Magnesium is stiff and a bit springy. I don't like aluminum in tanks, as I believe it poses a health risk we don't need to take.)

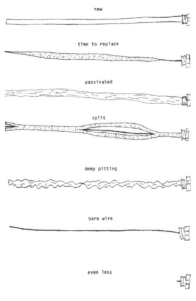

Is it a hex-head or a combination type? (If it's a hex-type that you use that 1-1/16″ socket on, that means you could add another anode in the hot port!)

Is there anything unusual about it? (Here we're looking for "passivation," which basically means the anode has stopped working.) Passivation is a hard coating of scale on the anode rod. The passivated anode will be pretty smooth and largely intact, even if it should be showing more signs of wear depending on age and water quality. Or the anode may show other stuff like the rod being split, or chunks of metal falling off. Those symptoms are common with aluminum anodes.

The ideal time to replace an anode is when 6″ of core wire is exposed. The rest of the rod should have even wear, and not be coated over with a hard calcium buildup, like the "time to replace" rod in the sketch.

Remove the Old Drain

This particularly can be a tricky job. You may want to find someone good with tools to do this. It's a good opportunity to watch and learn. If you're going to do it, use a crescent wrench and a square-shank basin wrench; you may also need a screwdriver, hammer, and rag. The first two tools are for removing the drain

Here is a typical plastic drain valve held by a basin wrench. A crescent wrench gives the needed force to unscrew the drain.

valve. The others are for removing any plastic remaining from the valve, and for preventing too much water from pouring out once that valve is removed. Of course, there is no rule against draining the heater first. That way you don't risk any water going where you don't want it going!

What sort of drain did the original equipment have? They often come with a simple plastic valve. The best drain is a full-port brass ball valve. Between the tank and valve, you want a lined steel nipple, and at the outlet of the valve you want a hose adaptor. Get these parts before even beginning to work on the tank.

What, if any, difficulties did you encounter in removing the old drain valve?

How big an opening is provided by that drain? (It's fun to try to look through some factory drain valves. With some, it's hard to see how water or sediment could ever get through!) A benefit of having a drain valve that can pass lots of water is that it can be used to help flush sediment from the tank, which is good. Typical factory drains often don't allow for flushing sediment out. Sometimes they clog up so the tank can't even be drained. These are reasons to have a good, full port drain valve.

Remove the Pipe Nipples On Top of the Tank

Use pipe wrenches, including the ratcheting type; you may also need a hammer and chisel.

What condition are the nipples in? Look for two things:

- Are the steel nipples clogged up with rust, slowing flow?
- Is there enough rust to weaken the threads, increasing the risk of leaks?

A trick for removing stubborn pipe nipples is to insert a 3/4″ steel rod into the nipple before torquing on it with your pipe wrench. This prevents the nipple from collapsing and likely tearing off. When one does tear off, it leaves a ring of rusty steel in the threaded port of the tank. This ring must come out so another nipple can go in, and that removal is a delicate job. You want to remove the ring without damaging the threads in the tank. This is where the hammer and chisel come into play. Use them to tap on an edge of the broken nipple and bend it inward. This loosens tension on the ring and then it can be unscrewed.

Remove the Dip Tube

Use channel locks. Stick one handle of the tool down into the dip tube, then wiggle it around while pulling up.

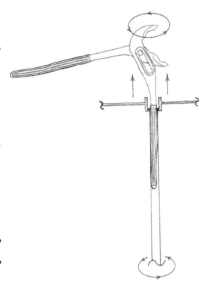

How does the dip tube look? Here you're looking for cracks in the plastic, or holes, or even some or all of the tube being broken off and missing.

If so, the cold incoming water will mix with the hot and give you a lukewarm shower. That's not fun, so if you find any of these conditions, replace the dip tube.

Try the T&P (Temperature and Pressure Relief Valve) Lever to See How It Feels, then Remove It

Use a pipe wrench.

Look up inside of the T&P relief valve to assess the amount of sediment or scale build-up.

Blow through the valve while the lever on it is open. If that doesn't work, then clearly a new valve is needed. This is really important, as the T&P relief valve is the last line of defense against the water heater blowing up if things go bad.

I've given you a lot of technical stuff here, and some of it even plumbers find challenging. If your eyes rolled back when reading any of this, it's just peachy to hire someone who has experience doing these things. Then watch closely and learn from them.

To wrap up, service, longevity, and safety are three things good water heater maintenance can give you. We want our equipment to work and deliver as much hot water as we need. We do not want the heater to leak on holiday mornings, and we especially want the equipment to be safe. Unsafe water heaters can shock us with 240 volts, leak carbon monoxide gas into our homes, scald us with too-hot water, grow bacteria inside with too-cool water, leak and cause all sorts of damage, or simply blow up with amazing force. Good maintenance prevents all of that and saves money, too. I've seen well-maintained tanks last for over fifty years! Pretty good.

There's a lot more information on the art and science of hot water at www.waterheaterrescue.com.

Clues a Water Heater Gives You

If only we would listen, our water heaters have a lot to tell us. Much like people, water heaters don't appreciate not being heard. Why do you think heaters fail on holidays and weekends? They want attention! Most folks only pay attention when their water heater has failed—on Christmas morning or at some other inconvenient time.

If a water heater feels REALLY neglected, it can do much worse than just stop working; it can even kill us via carbon monoxide, fire, or explosion. If you want to avoid such unhappy predicaments, here are a few things you can do.

First, just have an admiring glance at the water heater periodically. Has anything changed? Is there rust or moisture anywhere? If it's a gas-fired water heater, is the vent pipe still hooked up? Is there a drain line from the temperature-

and-pressure relief valve, and is it piped to a safe location? Is the end of that pipe dry? Is anything stored on top of or right next to your gas water heater? I've seen fire caused by a broom left too close to the combustion chamber.

Next, it pays to understand why water heaters die. The most common form of neglect is failing to replace the sacrificial anode rod (called this because the magnesium or aluminum rod gets sacrificed to protect the steel tank). When the anode has been used up, there is no longer any rust protection for the steel tank. Water heaters just love having new anodes! It may be difficult to remove an old, stubborn anode, but it's far less work than replacing the whole water heater. The anode will tell you more about the condition of the tank than anything else, so it is worth the trouble of getting it out. You might want to have a look online at WaterHeaterRescue.com for a lot more info on replacing anodes—and most anything else about water heaters! Also, you can simply do an online search for "anode replacement water heater." There is plenty of information available on the subject of anodes.

The next water heater killer is pressure. Just like you and me, water heaters really hate to be under too much pressure. If water pressure gets too high, or if it fluctuates rapidly, this can cause the glass lining of the tank to crack and flake off, leaving bare steel to rust. Ideally, you want water pressure to be in the 40-60 psi range (psi = pounds per square inch). Get an inexpensive 0-200 psi gauge and measure the water pressure in your water heater. The drain valve is a good place to take the measurement. Also, watch the gauge when water is heating, and no water is running. One type of gauge has a little red pointer that shows you the highest pressure the gauge has seen. If the water pressure creeps up higher than the static pressure (static is when no water is being used), you know that thermal expansion from heating the water is raising the water pressure in the entire house. (This is common in homes that have pressure-reducers or backflow preventers.) Sometimes there is a check valve in the water meter. If that relief valve drips periodically, it could be a clue that the water pressure is too high. Most temperature-and-pressure relief valves open at 150 psi, so periodic dripping tells you that the water heater is suffering from too much pressure. But if the relief valve doesn't drip, it doesn't necessarily mean that all is well. In my area, roughly one out of forty relief valves is plugged solid with minerals due to water hardness; it's like capping the line, leaving you with no protection at all. One in forty is too much like Russian roulette for me! If a relief valve is plugged, one possible consequence is that the water heater explodes—and they go off with a **lot** of force! A thirty-gallon tank exploding is like setting off two sticks of dynamite. You'll see at WaterHeaterRescue.com just how to test a relief valve so that you can know if it's working.

Sediment buildup in a tank is also not a good thing. It's the heater's version of indigestion. Imagine how bloated you would feel if you had all that sediment in you! In gas water heaters, sediment slows heat transfer, causing overheating at the bottom and dissolving the glass lining. In gas water heaters, sediment can also trap water, which then boils and makes a rumbling noise. In electric water heaters, sediment can bury and burn out the lower element, as well as providing a cozy breeding ground for bacteria. WaterHeaterRescue.com offers flushing parts you can install in your water heater to help reduce the problem. Unlike humans, water heaters aren't fond of getting all sedimental.

Heaters like to breathe too! Gas-fired water heaters can give clues about how their venting systems are working—or not. On top of the water heater is a "draft hood," which exhausts combustion byproducts to the outside via a vent pipe. Sometimes, if air pressures are wonky, you'll see discoloration on the pipe nipples that live on both sides of the draft hood. If these nipples are rusty on one side, or if their insulation has melted, you know there is a venting issue. Additionally, if you see evidence of overheating toward the bottom of the heater, in front under the control valve, that's another reason to check out the venting. This evidence will look like paint discolored from the heat, or rusting on the side of the tank. Having a carbon monoxide detector in the house just might not be a bad idea either! If the detector goes off, it's a clue that the water heater isn't "breathing" correctly.

Sometimes a water heater that's feeling neglected will just stop giving you all the hot water you want. The solution could be a simple thermostat adjustment; thermostats do drift with time. But it could also indicate a damaged dip tube. The dip tube is a plastic pipe inside the tank that delivers cold water to the bottom, where it won't mix with the hot water. These dip tubes can get brittle with age and crack or fall off. The only way to know for sure is to unhook the cold line on top and pull the dip tube up and out of the tank to have a look.

But sometimes the problem has nothing to do with the water heater. A crossover in the plumbing (a leak from hot to cold or vice versa) can make it look like the water heater is ill or in a bad mood. By mixing cold water into the hot water, a crossover can fool people into looking for the problem in the wrong place. If you shut off the water supply to your water heater and open a hot faucet, the hot water should stop running in a few seconds. If it keeps running, there is a plumbing problem—and the water heater can remain happily blameless.

There are, of course, many other ways in which water heaters can fail, but these are the most common things that go wrong. With the knowledge I've shared here, your water heater can get the attention it wants, live a long and contented life, and give you hot water whenever you wish. Your water heater really would much rather live happily than resort to thinking murderous or leaky thoughts. If you listen carefully to that water heater you just maintained, you might even hear it say, "Tanks!"

Water Heater Safety and Installation Problems

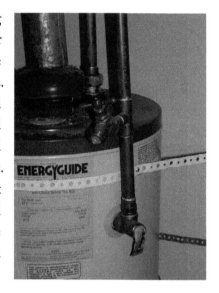

This is simply a cheat sheet for getting to the root of tank-type water heater problems quickly. I've broken the checklist items into three categories. First are problems that affect all common water heaters, followed by gas water-heater problems, and then electric water-heater problems. The picture here shows at least six different features that we could call "interesting." Have a look and see what you think they are. I'll tell you what I see at the end. 😌

All Water Heaters

T&P (temperature-and-pressure relief valve) clogged—cannot function, so tank could explode!

T&P date code years before date code on water heater—old T&P reused; violates code

T&P has steel fitting in it—dissimilar metal contact could rust and restrict flow

T&P drain line size reduced—code no-no

T&P drain line running uphill—code and gravity say must drain down

T&P mounted on fitting away from tank—will not sense temperature correctly, tank go boom!

T&P drain line made from PVC—cannot take the heat

PVC pipe run to heater—cannot take heat, gonna leak

Galvanized steel nipples used in tank—not durable in many waters

Brass nipples used in tank—will accelerate rusting of tank

Brass bibb used to replace cheap plastic drain—will also accelerate rusting of tank

Shutoff valve installed at cold pipe nipple on top of tank—no union downstream of shutoff…how do you service it?

Shutoff valve on left side of tank—might put dip tube at hot outlet, reversing flow direction; not good for your shower! (Dip tube is a pipe inside the tank that delivers cold water to the bottom.)

Water stains on top of water heater—suggests overhead pipe or valve leak—or rain coming down vent pipe!

Hot water delivery problems—possibly because of dip tube in wrong place or missing

Water heater sitting in drain pan with capped drain line—it happens!

Gas Water Heaters

Soot on flue or combustion chamber—suggests poor combustion, which means carbon monoxide is in the air you might be breathing!

Soot outside of combustion chamber access—poor draft, could be airflow problems at air inlet, exhaust, or flow obstruction in heater

Melted, heat-damaged gas control—really poor draft, or missing access cover(s)

Discoloration on interior side of pipe nipples at tank top—evidence of backdrafting, which occurs when combustion gas spills out rather than going up the vent

Melted pipe insulation on interior side at draft hood—combustion gas spilling

Rusty or gritty water-heater top around draft hood—combustion gas spilling

Draft hood has legs bent out to fit long vent pipe—will alter draft and could overheat vent pipe; hoods should never be modified from their original configuration

Vent pipe not screwed to draft hood—can come loose

Holes rusted through vent pipe—a place to leak gasses, suggests condensation and a poor draft

Vent pipe enlarged as it leaves water heater—will reduce vent's ability to exhaust gasses

Vent pipe running level or downhill—makes for poor or no draft and corroded pipe

Pile of rusty flakes on burner—corrosive air (contains chemicals) being burned (eg: chlorine)

High-limit contacts removed from thermocouple connection—no high-limit protection; human error!

Electric Water Heaters

Plastic covers missing from 240 volt electric water heater thermostats —a bad place for fingers

Dual-element water heater wired for simultaneous operation—can overload supply wiring

Electric thermostat/high limit not tight to tank so it cannot sense true tank temperature—heater at risk of explosion!

No insulation over thermostats—results in inaccurate temperature reading

Metal covers not fully affixed over thermostats—exposed 240 volts—bad place for kids

Wattage on element different from name tag—heating too slow or fast, drawing too much

Bare Romex going into tank—unprotected wiring, baaad!

Undersized supply wiring—can overheat, burn down house!

Wire nuts at connection too small—poor junction, can come off

Now, about that photo of an "interesting" water heater. What stands out first to me is that the relief-valve line goes up. That's a no-no; it causes the valve to stay wet and to corrode shut. The plumber tried to do a workaround by installing a hose bibb above it, but no cigar! The drain line needs to drain down. That's two problems.

How about that plumbers-tape earthquake strap? It will work fine until there's an earthquake. There just isn't enough metal to hold that tank full of water. Use an engineered strap kit.

Next are those unions just above the tank (called dielectric unions). Experienced plumbers avoid them because they fill with rust, restrict flow, and are a pain to mess with. Note that these have copper pipe above and brass nipples below, which will make the unions rust even more quickly. That's four.

Then look at those nice brass nipples. They are better than plain steel, but they are screwed into a steel tank, which will rust to protect the nipples (not good!). It would be better to use plastic-lined steel nipples. This prevents galvanic corrosion at the pipe connections. Even better would be to use flex connectors between those lined nipples and the copper pipe. This can give you a true dielectric connection that doesn't rust shut.

Finally, see the red shutoff valve handle at the top of the tank? It's a gate valve. This was once the only real choice, but these days we have ball valves, which don't snap off in your hands when you try to use them, and you can tell by looking if they are open or closed—simpler and better. Just make sure you use "full port" valves, or you might inadvertently reduce water flow. That's six, and I haven't even said a thing about replacing the sacrificial anode, or the fact that there is no insulation on the pipes!

Hot Water Heaven

It's easy to imagine ideal hot-water systems, but not so easy to find them in the real world. There are too many compromises in cost, quality, expectation, and education. Money and ego play a part as well. In my dream, we would have long-lived, efficient systems that have minimal environmental impact. I'd like to daydream out loud for a bit, and share some "what could be" and "if only" thoughts as they relate to hot water.

The ideal water heating system would be supremely energy-and water-efficient. It would last as long as the building it was installed in. It would be a pleasure to live with. It would be absolutely safe and, of course, it wouldn't cost too much.

You're not going to get such an elegant system installed by a plumber who isn't thoroughly trained in hot water work (most aren't). Many plumbers are more interested in finishing your work fast and moving on to the next job, or are assuming that you only want the cheapest equipment. They aren't necessarily thinking about your long-term satisfaction. The challenge here is how to properly educate the workforce, not just in things technical, but also in business basics and management. With such an education, correctly trained plumbers wouldn't lose so much work to relatively unskilled (and possibly unsafe) workers.

Fortunately, when it comes to efficiency and longevity, we have many examples from the past to help show us the way. In 1906, there were condensing water heaters that claimed ninety-two percent efficiency (most modern gas-fired heaters are far less efficient, at around sixty percent). Since these were point-of-use heaters, there were no plumbing distribution losses, and little time was spent waiting for hot water. There were also "U" tube water heaters, which stopped much of the standby loss that gas water heaters suffer from. I go into more detail about these nice old water heaters in the article titled "How Efficient Can Old Technology Be?"

In my daydream, modern hot water engineers study old designs like these in order to incorporate the good ideas from the past into today's water heaters. I collected a bunch of interesting old water heaters, which the General Society of Mechanics and Tradesmen in New York has put on permanent display. Hopefully, this collection will serve as a resource for future hot water engineers and anyone else who's fanatical or simply interested in hot water.

Here's another gift from the past: Have you heard of Monel? It's a copper/nickel mix that is currently used for high-end boat fittings. From the 1930s through the 1950s, you could get water heaters made of Monel. These and copper tanks were often the last tank a homeowner would ever need to buy, but such long-lived tanks are essentially unavailable now. Roughly eighty-five percent of the nine million or so water heaters made yearly are sold as replacements. That's $13.5 billion! *not* chump change. The manufacturers seem convinced that low cost is the most important thing to buyers, so tanks that have proven to be long-lived are just a memory (there are exceptions, but they make up a tiny fraction of the market). My dream is that manufacturers compete in producing the highest-quality water heater, just as their predecessors did, instead of competing to make the cheapest water heater, which must be replaced with alarming regularity.

The cost of any hot water system needs to be put in perspective. Manufacturers and plumbers both compete on price, but how cost-effective is something that needs more servicing and frequent replacement? In my dream, end users would be educated in life-cycle costing, in which all costs over time are taken into account. This is the only way to know whether you're really getting a good deal. Government and other institutions could set a good example and help retrain the homeowning public. More demand for long-lived equipment would help make such equipment readily available at reasonable prices. Another benefit would be far less need to recycle or dump millions of used water heaters into our already overcrowded landfills.

Just as there are rating systems for energy performance in new construction, I'd like to see the same thing done for hot water systems, not simply the water heater. Ratings could be based on total energy use per person, waiting times for hot water, volume of water in the line between heater and fixture, and so on. This would motivate plumbers to do better than just meet code. My colleague Gary Klein is working on this concept with his "hot water rectangle," which is a way of looking at wet-room placement in a building and being able to see in general just how efficient it may be. Wet rooms are rooms with plumbing in them, like kitchens and bathrooms. The smaller the hot water rectangle is, the more energy- and water-efficient things will be, and you won't have to wait so long for hot water to arrive! Visit www. to garykleinassociates.com. to see more.

Let's look at some other areas in which attention to detail could make things better. Sediment creates problems in many modern water heaters, particularly those with aluminum anode rods. One fix from history could be the "external flue" heater. This model had a narrow flue wrapping completely around the tank, instead of the central flue common in modern water heaters. In addition to increased surface area for better heat transfer, this water heater allowed the lower tank head to be domed downward. The resulting shape would look like a normal supplement capsule, standing up on end. Sediment would collect at the low point in the center, then be easily removed by opening a drain valve attached there. With modern insulation, external-flue heaters would lose far less heat, making them less expensive to own and more desirable to use. We modern folks have to live with pounding and thumping in gas water heaters because sediment is so hard to remove from the bottom of today's tanks. Electric heaters don't make this racket because they aren't trying to heat water through a blanket of sediment. Aluminum anodes contribute to the problem of sediment by creating a great volume of corrosion byproduct. Magnesium anodes (although slightly more expensive) used to be the norm and don't make such a mess.

Here's another example: In my daydream, metal distribution piping that steals BTUs from the hot water and holds way too much water would be a relic of the inefficient past. One way to replace such a relic would be manifold plumbing. A manifold is like a "T" with many little ports on the side of the "T" instead of just one. Using a manifold allows you to run small-diameter tubing directly to each faucet or place where water will be used. Manifold systems using well-insulated 3/8″ PEX tubing (or even 1/4″ tubing for short runs) would be the norm for medium-sized and smaller homes. This method provides quick hot-water delivery, creates much less water waste, and is installed more like wiring than rigid pipe, making new construction simpler and retrofitting much easier.

The industry presently leans toward using electronics, pumps, and other active things to improve energy- and water-efficiency. But these things normally don't last for decades, and long-term reliability is one of my goals. For example, you can cut standby heat loss from an electric water heater by adding a time clock or by installing heavy insulation. I would opt for the "nothing to go wrong" insulation first. Of course, a timer could be added to keep the water heater turned off during periods of high electricity cost, but it's just one more thing to get thrown out of whack.

Water-heater manufacturers have also attempted to improve energy performance by paying a lot of attention to heater efficiency and insulation to keep the heat in the tank. But the way systems are built, much of that precious heat goes down the drain. We could capture much of that heat directly from the drain by using something called a drain heat exchanger. Once we look at the actual costs of our current practices, monetary and otherwise, employing such simple technologies makes better sense. There's another simple technology I've been keeping my eye on for some years: a non-electric flue damper. It is a simple, inexpensive device that fits under the draft hood and cuts standby losses by at least thirty percent. Now, if you put one of these dampers on an external-flue heater, you'd have one simple and high-performance water heater! But somehow the long and winding process of getting regulatory approvals—perhaps combined with egos and territorialism—have all conspired to keep the device off the market. It would be nice to see more regulators and industry representatives looking at the common good rather than at their own turf. I'd love to see the process of getting good and efficient equipment to market made simpler, faster, and far less expensive than it currently is. Maybe government-sponsored competitions designed to encourage the most efficient equipment design—and then help get this good stuff into the market—would be a good role for government regulatory agencies. As energy and clean water become increasingly expensive, such obstacles and turf wars need to become less relevant.

My daydreams aren't actually pessimistic. The necessary technology already exists. Together, we have the talent and muscle necessary to make efficient, safe, and easy-to-live-with water-heating systems a reality. We are only lacking consensus among the players.

 Do what you know is right, even if it's hard. You'll sleep better.

How Efficient Can Old Technology Be?

Here is a water heater that was made in 1895. That makes it about 127 years old. Certainly, we have much more energy-efficient equipment now, right? Well, only perhaps. This is a condensing water heater. It's also a "contact" heater. This means that flame and hot flue gasses mingle directly with the water being heated. In this water heater, water is streaming down through the same passages that fire and hot flue gasses are going up! Measurements of similar heaters have shown an energy efficiency of ninety-two percent. Your standard modern gas heater is more like sixty percent. Another interesting thing about this heater is that it has only three moving parts. There just isn't much to fail, and if it does, it's easy to fix.

Also, as you can see, it's made of copper. As long as water is not acidic or aggressive in some other way, this water heater won't fail from corrosion. It's a demand water heater that uses no electricity, and has no standing pilot flame, so it has no standby energy losses. All those ideas from one water heater called the Ewart's Royal Geyser!

I collect old water heaters, and at one time I had over seventy of them. Each one presents ideas. Some are good, like this one I've been discussing, and some demonstrate ideas that are surprisingly unsafe or uninformed.

Here's an example of a scary water heater from the 1920s. It's electric, but as you can see it has only two prongs; there is no ground. The ground is the third prong you see in a modern electrical plug. It helps keep any electricity from flowing through you! This water heater is designed to strap to the spout on the kitchen faucet. You turn on the tap, then plug it in, and you get a little stream of hot water from it. In those days, that was much better and faster than heating water on the stove. A plus to this sort of heater is there are no heat losses in the plumbing; it's a point-of-use heater and very efficient. The problems, however, are in starting it correctly: first water flow, then power…or it melts down! But the main problem is the lack of a ground. If you put one hand in the water and your other hand on a metal sink, guess what…you become the ground path for the electricity. That's why you don't see these anymore; they had a record of electrocuting children! Sometimes there's more to life than energy-efficiency.

Now have a look at this water heater: It's got the same heating element—Nichrome wire, exposed directly to the water—but it has two other things: a ground and a flow switch. This way, it can remain plugged in without using a person as a ground path. It's actually a water heater designed specifically for showering. The shower head mounts directly to the heating unit, so you get to wash with this device right there in the shower. In the U.S., we've been trained to keep anything electrical away from where we bathe, so this heater might take a little getting used to. Heck, in Great Britain they often use 240-volt showerheads! With this model, you still have no line or standby losses. Not bad for an old idea. These days, with grounding mandated in the electric code, maybe heaters like this could safely have a place.

As you're beginning to see, old water heaters offer up a treasure trove of ideas to consider. Here's a diagram of one such interesting design from the mid-1940s. See how the flue inside the tank heads up to the top, then turns 180° and heads back down to near the bottom before it exits out the side? Then you'll see the draft hood down near the base of the tank. This greatly reduces the standby energy loss from the tank, as the flue is no longer acting like a chimney and sucking air through the water heater, wasting heat all the time. This "U tube" design is essentially a heat trap for the flue, so flue gasses only flow when the main burner comes on. It saves lots of energy and has no moving

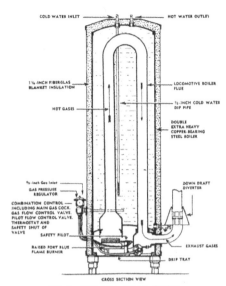

Fig. 1—"U" Tube Water Heater

parts. Also, it doubles the heat transfer area of the flue for more efficient utilization of heat from the flue gasses. Clearly this heater would cost a little more to make than the basic design used today. I can't think of any other reason for it not being used if you must have a gas fired water heater.

When electric water heaters were first made in the early 1900s, they didn't perform all that well, as the supply of electricity to homes was small by today's standards and the heating element might draw only 600 or 1000 watts. This means they heated water very slowly, seriously limiting how much hot water was available. Today, the common element size is 4,500 watts. The manufacturers got around the problem of slow recovery, or the inability to heat water quickly by adding a tempering tank.

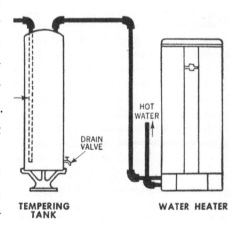

The basic idea was to place the uninsulated tank in a warm place, like a boiler room, a sunny place, or wherever there was "waste" heat available. Feeding the slow electric water heater with warm water made it more capable of meeting the demand, because it now had less work to do to be able to deliver adequately hot water. It probably also reduced complaints to the manufacturer. I see no reason why we can't do the same thing now and put some waste heat to use. By borrowing the best old ideas, it would not be difficult to build a water heater that is far more efficient than most modern models that will last as long as the house it's installed in, and will probably cost little more than a conventional water heater. Also, if we keep it very simple, the likelihood of it needing much upkeep is significantly reduced. Think of the savings this imaginary heater could provide over its long life! Finally, if we got used to thinking of life-cycle cost instead of first cost, we'd be willing to spend a bit more for this water heater because it should never need replacing. Food for thought!

Finding Mama Cat

Several years ago, I bought a run-down house in Salinas to rehab. For months, I worked to bring it back to being nice, attractive, warm, and secure (it was none of those things). In the large yard, many truckloads of trash had accumulated over the years. The trash had to go; broken concrete, tires, barbed wire, and broken glass don't make for a happy home—unless you're a wild cat.

My workmate, Tim, first met Mama Cat when he started to clear out one pile of trash. She was camped out there with a litter of obviously newborn

kittens. Their eyes were closed, and their ears were flat, suggesting they were only a few days old.

We didn't want to disturb this new family, so Tim moved on to other projects and I started feeding Mama Cat; she was just fur, skin, and bones! After some days, I formed a plan in my head to relocate Mama and her brood to a nice, warm, towel-lined box, thinking she would like it better than a dirt floor in a pile of trash. First, I moved the kittens (there turned out to be nine). I knew that it's good for kittens to stay with their mom for at least a month so they can get the benefits of her milk, so I hoped she would follow.

Mama was not thrilled. She moved half of them back to the trash heap. The others were crying for Mama, so I moved them closer to her—and back into the trash heap they went. My plan had failed.

So I stopped and simply watched. Then I noticed an unhappy thing. One by one, kittens were vanishing. Hawks were living in the big eucalyptus trees close by. I felt I had to act for the benefit of the remaining kittens. I moved all five into a box and went shopping for kitty supplies. I was gone for about 45 minutes, and when I came back there were only four kittens left: two tabbies, a black one, and a black-and-white. I had to enact my plan fast.

I could never get closer to wild Mama than about 100 feet; she wanted nothing to do with me. So I took all the kittens home and started bottle-feeding them every three hours. They weighed four to five ounces at the time.

The next day, I took the kittens to the vet for a checkup. The vet cleaned them up a bit and treated each kitten's umbilical wound. I thought we were good to go.

But things went downhill pretty fast from there. In two days, the kitties were lethargic. I called the vet and brought them in. One tabby was gone before I arrived. When I got there, they told me that the remaining tabby had no hope and should be put down. The last two had fevers, so they were given antibiotics and fluids. I was surprised how much it hurt to lose the two tabbies. A few days later, the black kitten started going cold like the tabbies  had, and I did what I could to keep him warm by holding him against me and keeping the car heater cranked up. At home, I added a hot water bottle and a microwaved rice bag to my bag of kitten-warming tricks. And it worked!

I needed to keep the two surviving kittens close to me so that I could feed them often, but I also had to get back to work. So those kittens essentially grew up close to me in my car; it's a mobile home for them.

The whole time I was working on the Salinas house, I kept an eye out for Mama Cat, but no sightings. My two kitties were growing, playing, and learning how to maneuver in the big world.

One day, I came up with the idea of gaining their trust by keeping them close and carrying them around upside-down in my arms. It worked, and we got along just fine. I weighed them daily, as that seems to be the measure of how well a kitten is doing. When I needed to go out of town for a few days, a friend offered to care for them. I felt very protective of my two remaining kitties, so I bugged her for daily reports of kitty weight. They did fine in my absence.

One day at the Salinas house, I spotted Mama Cat with three black-and-white kittens following her. So, we had each lost two. They were wild, and would run off even if I was far away, but I fed them. So work progressed on the house, I left food out, and Mama Cat sightings happened.

Three kitties became two, and then there were no more kitty sightings. One day, when my kitties were four months old, I was packing up to go home and took one last look in the yard. On the neighbor's property, I saw Mama Cat and a plastic cup moving around. A kitten had stuck its head in the cup and couldn't get it off. Mama could only watch, helpless.

I jumped the fence, scooped up the kitten, cut off the cup, and was pleased to see the kitten eat a little from the dish I'd left nearby. It was a sad-looking kitten, with a gray face, eyes mostly glued shut and oozing pus, and bones showing under the thin skin. I took him home and bathed him, got good medicine for his eyes, bathed him again, and fed him. He weighed one pound four ounces. (His brother weighed five pounds four ounces at the time.)

The vet found fleas, worms, and infection. In this kitten's first days with me, he simply sat; he acted like an old cat in pain. But he got better. Over time, he lost much of his wildness, and no longer ran for cover every

time I walked into the room. He never got as big as his brothers, but he played with them and jumped on them like he didn't know the difference. Maybe he was making up for lost play time.

Before naming the kitties, I waited for each one to demonstrate their personality so that I could determine each one's right and fitting name. The first black-and-white is named Rex, because he clearly is the boss and is regal about it.

Shadow is the black one (he's actually a dark tabby; if seen in sunlight, his stripes and swirls appear). He sits and figures things out quietly and inscrutably. I suspect he does calculus for entertainment.

The recent addition (who is also black and white) is Watcher. I had to put a bell on him to have any hope of finding him. Otherwise, he'd just sit or hide, quietly invisible. Last time I weighed them all, Rex was  seven pounds, Shadow was a bit over six pounds, and Watcher was five pounds. They all became happy, healthy kitties, turning into cats. Change is inevitable. Tim and I finished up the Salinas house. Mama Cat got used to my feeding her, but she had no intention of leaving the neighborhood. I felt that she was now my responsibility, so I had some weighty questions to consider: Should I leave her to have more kittens who'd be unlikely to survive? Should I catch her, have her fixed, and return her to the wild? Or should I catch her and bring her home to live with her three healthy offspring? In her diary, coming up, let's see what Mama Cat says about all that…

Living World

My Love Affair with Water

Water and I go way back. I've always enjoyed playing with, watching, feeling, hearing, and being near water. As a small kid, I made little dams in the flow of water by the side of the road as it rained. That taught me about how to build dams that curved towards the incoming water to  use water pressure to make the dam stronger. I grew up in sight of the Pacific Ocean and could always hear the distant roar of waves breaking; particularly at night when there was less human-made noise. If I went to the right place on the peninsula where I lived, I could get that quiet roar from three sides. It was great fun jumping from stone to stone at the water's edge, making sure I didn't land on kelp as it can be pretty slippery. I knew that I had to respect kelp and what it can do to an unaware kid. As a Cub Scout, I built my first wooden boat, learning something about woodworking techniques and tricks. I took that boat around to nearby lakes and streams and got pretty good at rowing long distances in it. I still have a strong back because of that early exercise. Later, I turned it into a glass bottomed boat so I could better see what was happening deep in the water below.

In high school, I got certified in scuba diving. The equipment back then was pretty crude compared to today's gear, but it worked. I was scuba diving in the ocean at fifteen. I did some night dives and saw a very different world than what was out there during the day. I made equipment, like a dive light, so I could see the real colors of things down at 120 feet and built an electric "scooter" to drag me around underwater. There are some images in my head that are just unforgettable, like coming face to face with a wolf eel, with his huge jaws and pointy teeth, or being in water so clear that I could see a horizon, probably 300 feet away. Diving in Hawaii, I remember waving to people in the glass-bottomed boat that had dropped me off. I was eighty feet down at the time and could see them clearly. Water clarity varies. I remember running into the ocean bottom with my mask during another dive because the water was so green and murky.

Being underwater is good, but I liked being on it, as well, so I learned how to sail. Sailing is an old art. It encourages you to understand natural forces and properties of materials. You learn about the strength of things and how to work with rope, from knots to splicing. You also learn what saltwater does to metals and how to protect and preserve those metals. It makes you pay attention to the little nuances and whispers the wind and water send you. In my early twenties, I got a twenty-five-foot sailboat and ranged up and down the coast in various weather conditions. Sometimes the wind would vanish and other times it would try to knock the boat over. One time, I was about ten miles out to sea and a pod of four orcas spotted me. I could see the dorsal fins of the two males, roughly six feet tall, and one fin had a bend near the tip, like he'd run into something. The male orcas were longer and certainly heavier than my boat. And they were curious! The four of them crossed directly under my boat, missing it by just a few feet. My adrenalin was working just fine, thank you! They continued silently on their way. Sailing along the coast at night, I'd need to listen carefully for the sounds of the breakers to make sure I wasn't too close to shore. Then I took a leap and crewed on larger sailboats going from California to Hawaii and back. Sailors call the open ocean "blue water." Spending twenty-five days in a thirty-six-foot boat on blue water, at times 1,000 miles from land, gives such a different perspective on space and time than we can get "in town." The rhythms at sea are very different! Watching a line squall coming at you, where you go from sunny and calm to knocked-over mayhem in thirty seconds, gets your attention. Being on the tail end of a hurricane, where you need to dodge twenty-foot breaking waves, keeps you alert and present. Thing is, the worse the weather, the stronger my focus on paying attention to everything around me became. Fear was never part of the equation, as there was no room for it. It doesn't help. This is another gift the water has given me. These days I simply go kayaking when I find the time. It still feels great to be on the water!

I started tinkering with mechanical things before I was ten. I just wanted to know how they all worked. At first, I'd take things apart. After a while I figured out how to put them back together, which my parents seemed to think was a good thing. So, then I got to mix up my love of the water and all things mechanical. Dripping faucets please nobody, so I learned the basics of repairing them. Fortunately, I've had good mentors along the way. If you want to learn something badly enough, a mentor will show up and help you. It just works that way, and you can be confident this is true. That's how I learned about hot water and water heaters. I really wanted to know more about how water heaters worked than I could learn through books or asking around in the United States, but eventually was given the name of a man in Canada who had a deep understanding of the whole subject. Eventually we were both members of the same committee on corrosion engineering and how it related to hot water. I learned a lot and hopefully gave some knowledge back in that relationship.

Water, in her own way, has been my longest-term mentor. Water has steadily been teaching me, nearly my entire life. She has been creative in how she teaches and when. Water only gives what I'm able to take in and put to use. One lesson I've learned is that she does demand respect. If you fail in that way, it can cost you dearly. I was a slow learner, and it took nearly drowning a few times before I finally understood her tough love.

Having hot water is a great example of how we don't even notice something when it's doing its job well. If I were a great writer, you would hardly notice these words, because you would be so engaged in the story they tell. Good hot water service is like that. We simply expect it when we open the tap. It arrives and isn't given a second thought, until it doesn't arrive! Then, life isn't so good. When we have plenty of hot water, there can be peace in the house. We get the long shower, clean dishes and clothes, and maybe even the luxuriant tub bath. This all gives up time and space to think and feel about the good things in life, and even get philosophical and appreciative of the many gifts the world gives us to experience. Take away that hot water and we're often not so pleased with life. There is something (probably expensive) to fix and unhappy time spent making or waiting for the fix to happen. There may be damage caused by leaking, making the problem much bigger. No doubt you've heard stories about people having no hot water. Heaters do like to fail at the most inconvenient times!

I like being helpful. It just seems to be how I'm wired. So, imagine life with no plumbing or mechanical problems. Imagine the peacefulness. Imagine the lack of worry. Imagine spending your time getting to simply enjoy what the world offers up, without the distraction brought on by mechanical difficulties. This is one connection between the philosophical and the mechanical worlds. The mechanical can facilitate the philosophical, making it easier to get there, stay there, and enjoy.

With all that mechanical worry out of the way, it becomes easier to find time and space to consider water in her many aspects. Water as a means of keeping us healthy or giving us comfort is one. Water as a connection between us and the rest of life on Earth, past and present, is another. Even in her unique way, water as a true lifeform, being powerful, generous, and wise, is one that begs us to slow down, put on our philosopher's hats and simply enjoy! While we usually put up a wall between the worlds of mechanical and philosophical things, I think it time to have another look and understand that they aren't separate at all, but rather two sides of the same coin. They fit together perfectly, like Yin and Yang.

Growing Old?

I'm quickly getting close to having been on our planet for seventy years. Still, occasionally I ride a motorcycle or have fun climbing a tree. Much more often you'll find me in an attic or tight crawl space fixing something. I'm not good at acting my age, it seems. Just when I should be feeling old, frail, and creaky, I'm working on a book or solving somebody's problems or just itching to go sea kayaking.

We refer to ourselves as x-years old, never x-years young. It feels like we're programming ourselves to die at around eighty. A doctor named Naram, part of the 2500-year-old healing lineage of Siddha Veda, had a master named Baba Ramdas who lived to 125. He made it so far in full control; no creeping decrepitude for him! This master's master made it to 145 years young, we're told. Interestingly, it was just in the news that the human body is capable of making it up to 150! That's what modern science is telling us. So, why should we be preparing to die at a little over half that age?

I used to think I'd be surprised if I made it to seventy. But imagine how you would live life if you expected to, or simply didn't rule out the possibility of, being around for 150 years! At fifty or sixty, you wouldn't be planning your retirement, you'd be thinking about traveling and learning more, or doing those good things that you're now prepared and able to do better than ever. You might be looking forward to sharing some pearls of wisdom and some fun with your great, great (great?), grandkids. Age wouldn't weigh heavily on you, but rather, it would lift you up, propelled by experience and wisdom.

Now imagine that you only make it to eighty, but were planning on 149 and a half. Those latter years of your life would have been forward looking, useful, and happy, not simply a preparation for leaving. Isn't that a far nicer way to live? Is there a downside to keeping the door open to the possibility of 150 years? I'm not suggesting that you don't write a will until you're 120, but rather know that you can have so many more good years than we generally expect. Of course, this means that to take advantage of all that bonus time we need to learn more about how to take care of our bodies, minds, and spirits. It doesn't work just to take care of the body. We want and need the whole package! After all, they are intimately interconnected. These three are only yours to own, take care of, and be rewarded by.

Think about how we are trying to care for our planet. The science is clear that if we allow "business as usual" to proceed, we'll come quickly to a tipping point, and from there things get bad quickly. Many people are working hard to back us down from that point and avoid the destruction it would bring. We're learning quickly how to respect and maintain the health of the planet.

Think about your own health and what the stakes are with "business as usual." Let's make time to learn how to thrive and know that you will be generously rewarded for your efforts. It's literally a two for one. You'll get two "lifetimes" to live well. There is nothing lost in hoping for this outcome, and then acting to make it happen. With some skill and a little luck, let's see how things are about the time we roll into the twenty-second century. Just imagine that perspective! Giant tortoises, who live to 150 years young, have it, and science now adds its voice in saying we can have that perspective, too.

What Do You See?

When you get the chance to look at wildlife outside your window, what do you see? I was just watching two young deer. A small male with little bumps for horns, and an even smaller female. There were a few crows, as well. Birdseed was waiting for everyone on the ground and there was water, too. The male deer just crunched down seed while the female sniffed at the water but didn't drink. She was reluctant to go near the spot by the seed where a crow was lingering. Finally, she found her nerve and the crow hopped two steps away, keeping an eye on her. The male just ate, seemingly unperturbed by crows or anything else. Hopefully the very aware female survives this world, carrying the burden of her heightened sensitivity… Other humans might have watched the scene and thought, "Mmm, venison!"

So much of what's real in the world depends on who is experiencing it and what their background is. It certainly depends on our ability to be quiet inside and fully present in the right here and now. Anticipation, expectations, memories, dreams, and logic all want to take us down their own paths, taking us out of the here and now. Quieting the mind and emotions, and allowing the world to give while simply receiving, is something babies are probably much better at than grownups. Methinks we need to study that art and get it back into our lives. Imagine how much better we could get along with others if we saw and agreed on some basic facts and truths! Imagine us all seeing and living in the same world!

Of course, this will probably never happen, because we'll always have different backgrounds and experiences; good, bad, or otherwise. However, the upside is that we'll always have opportunities created when we want to understand different perspectives. To me, this is a rich vein to be found and enjoyed. There is danger in just having your own experience, knowing all else is wrong, and being diverted by multiple "shiny objects" so much that you never develop your own sense of what's true and meaningful.

A world where we have the ability to know what others know, whether it's a human or some other animal…a world where we can turn that valve and throttle down the flow of internal noise which influences how and what we see, feel, and understand…and a world where we know how to use all of our senses to be completely in and with this world, undistracted, and focused. That sounds like a world of harmony, joy, and appreciation of and for life! That's what I see. ☻

Walking With Dan

I've known Dan for a long time. He wrote an article years ago talking about the smell of old books. I couldn't help but write to him (long before the internet), as I know and like that particular fragrance. We've stayed in touch as his career and mine both grew and evolved. We've watched each other's challenges and accomplishments while supporting each other in different ways. I remember years ago sitting with him and his wife in a diner. He was telling me about his world-changing plans. His wife giggled happily at the seemingly crazy thoughts. I thought then, and for many years, "What a wonderful relationship they have!"

Dan is just a bit older than I am, but he looks much younger. While my white hair is sparse, his hair is dark and full. I think it's because he smiles more! We're both in pretty good shape. I stay physically active, crawling around in attics, basements, and the occasional tree. He does it by walking miles every day. I went walking with him around his neighborhood and he showed me the sights. He knows all the sights, sounds, and people! He'd tell me about the neighborhood's antics—a remodel here, a romance there, and the lovely statuary partly hidden behind those shrubs. He's got stories about everything, as he collects stories the way some people collect coins. The stories are all different, but like coins, have similarities. His stories are also vibrantly alive.

Dan is a very sensitive man. He notices things that others don't. Also, as a student of history, he's able to see long-term trends and put things together in ways that those who don't know our past can never hope to do. Throw in that sensitivity, and you get a man who cares deeply, understands deeply, and knows how to gently encourage others to be their best. Much of his encouragement is done through setting a good example. He's got the ability to be present, right here and now. He shows others how to listen and respond with empathy. Those are becoming rare attributes. Dan knows the value of acceptance and doesn't let fear take control. Just being the way he's learned to be is useful and educational for those who can slow down enough to notice.

Dan lives on the East Coast, far from me, where I visited him just a few years ago. Unfortunately, I was silly enough to have a kidney stone then. I promise that you *never* want to deal with a kidney stone. I've dealt with all sorts of pain, but there is no pain quite like a kidney stone. Dan and his wife made me their top priority, put me up, and found the right stuff to help me get better. I'm normally quite self-sufficient, but had no problem letting go and letting them watch over me. It's so rare and nice to be able to trust someone that much.

We are both members of a society where the members are called Brother or Sister. I'm there because of Dan, but for me, this is far more than a symbolic naming. Dan, to me, is part of my chosen family, and that's just the best. There is no sticking together just because we should. We stay because we value each other, want the best for each other, and will do whatever it takes to support each other.

Walking with Dan around his neighborhood, and down the path of life, has made me a richer, better person. I'm optimistic that I've been good for him, as well. And by the way, he has changed the world! He's proven that dreaming big can work! That's the great man I get to call Brother.

 You are here for a reason. Find out what that reason is.

It's a Red Sock Day!

Many years ago, I worked at a fancy girls' school. The girls often didn't care much about pinching pennies so would toss out perfectly good stuff. My boss decided that I needed to learn how to dumpster dive to "save" the good stuff from the landfill.

He just loved pulling out little paper bags, because often they had change in them and he knew firsthand about living a hardscrabble life. But I was simply interested in a pair of red socks that looked particularly good because my socks had holes forming and needed darning.

I've long preferred wearing practical black socks, seeing no need to draw attention to my feet. So, I saved the red socks and put them away, but one morning when I went to get some socks, the red ones called out to me. They said, "If you wear us, you'll have a great day."

I thought, "OK you're on!"

So, I put them on and went about my day. It was a fine day indeed, filled with good surprises! From then on when I got the hunch that it would be a wonderful day, I'd wear the red socks. I never put them on to make sure, or force having a good day, I just wore them because the magic in the air told me it would be good.

Sometimes years go by and I don't put them on, and I can still have good days. But when the socks offer themselves up to be worn, and the feeling is right, it never fails in unpredictable and unexpected ways that

I have a good day. Maybe wearing them opens my mind more clearly to all the good that's around, just waiting to be noticed.

Thinking about the difference between weekend days and workdays, I'm wondering if wearing red socks during the workweek might help make it feel more like the weekend. Maybe we could take much of the drudgery and difficulty out of workdays by letting red socks help us see the good more easily during the week. Hmmm, maybe we could adopt a red sock state of mind much or all of the time. Imagine how the stress and anxiety would have no choice but to melt away! I could be doing difficult work in a nasty crawl space, but that red sock attitude might just make it enjoyable.

And imagine how having red socks on the brain could help with difficult people! You know those people. They might even be relatives, but if you have your red sock attitude going and simply know things are going to be surprisingly good, any barbs they throw at you aren't going to get through and hurt you. They might even feel good! Those red socks can be a powerful force for good. Maybe I'll get a backup pair!

Taking Care

This morning, I fed and watered the birds, rabbits, and deer. I fed and petted the cats and tended to my friend's damaged wrist. Yesterday I spent most of the day helping my brother, who is having problems walking and taking care of himself and his  house. He was clearly scared to walk without holding onto something, so I was his cane. I bandaged his legs, took him on errands, like shopping and a doctor visit, and trimmed his toenails, because he can't do it himself. I also helped out a couple of friends with technical questions around plumbing design and hot water stuff. Of course, I fed the animals yesterday, too. That is an everyday kinda thing. That's how my days roll sometimes, and I don't mind at all.

There are times when I don't get my own things done because I see others' needs as more pressing than mine. There's an internal scale that I hope lets me know when things are too out of balance, and when that happens I adjust, give myself time to do or to rest, and rebalance. That scale watches my time, of course, but it also tracks my energy, satisfaction, efficiency, stress, and just how present I am in the now. My scale weighs all this and guides me to what's next.

Fortunately, I'm not into keeping score, because if I was, I'd be deep in debt. The gifts the wildlife and my cats give me are worth so much more than a little seed and time! The comfort and reassurance my friends and brother get by knowing that I'm there for them, and the subsequent gratitude, give me a mix of peace, satisfaction, and quiet joy that can't carry a price tag.

Caretaking does seem to be an undervalued endeavor in my corner of the Western world. It's particularly apparent when someone gets Alzheimer's disease or some other form of brain illness. Friends usually stay away in droves, becoming distant when they are needed the most. Family has a hard time finding time to come help out or even to visit. The work of caring for an elderly parent often falls to one of their children, or the parent is put in an institution.

There are a number of caregiver support groups online. The stories of abandonment and of how invisible the caregivers feel are surprising and sad. They almost never get to take time off or do self-care. Many take years to recover once their "loved one" has left. I write about it here just to shine a light where darkness lives now.

In other parts of the world, this "taking care" falls under the term "seva," a Sanskrit word meaning selfless service. A smart man named Ram Dass explained it like this: "Helping out is not some special skill. It is not the domain of rare individuals. It is not confined to a single part of our lives. We simply heed the call of that natural impulse within and follow it where it leads us."

What I do by taking care can't compare to the magnitude of what full-time caregivers live with, but what we all do is to help the world go 'round. We take care of those many little seemingly unimportant tasks that really do have to get done to protect or enhance the quality of life for somebody, human or otherwise. Sometimes the only compensation is knowing that we're doing the right thing, but to me, that's far more meaningful than being in the spotlight of recognition or glory.

What the Animals Do for Me

Sitting on the deck outside with hummingbirds zooming around, deer walking by or napping under a nearby tree, quail, doves, juncos, and many other animals makes it clear that the right place for me to be is present. I don't want to miss noticing that ruby glint off the hummingbird in the sun, or the ways deer play, or the intent look on the face of the bobcat as he intently watches a flock of quail nearby. Then, back indoors, there is this demanding cat in my lap as I type. He wants all of that attention I'm giving to the keyboard!

The animals politely encourage me to be right here, right now, and that's a useful and amazing gift! I do have to bribe some of them with food for the privilege of their presence (or presents?), but it's a small price. Our world is a highly nuanced place, and being present allows me to pick up on things that could easily be missed and not appreciated. We humans are just too busy too much of the time. Even if we're sitting quietly, all those many thoughts bumping around in our heads focus our attention inward, so we can miss what's quietly happening all around. Just sitting quietly seems to be painful for a lot of folks. We turn on the TV or radio or look at some screen seemingly to avoid that deep, dark quiet. What scary monsters live in that quiet place? What hurts have we suffered that we keep locked up in there, just out of sight or consciousness?

Clearing space and creating pure, uncluttered time can be an intimidating proposition. I never know who or what will come to visit when I open the "quiet time" door. Thoughts and feelings always seem to come flooding in from unexpected places when there is a spot for them to roost. So, opening up a place for the animals could also bring the uninvited guests of real or imagined memories past. Even so, I find it's worth the risk because the animals give me unforgettable gifts. Have you ever had a hummingbird sit on your finger? When it happens to you, you'll never forget! I'm still working on enticing the deer to eat seed from my hand. I can almost feel that warm, fuzzy muzzle on my palm, along with the moist breath.

Being who I am, I like to have solutions for problems, and unfortunately, I don't have a quick, easy one for having an overly-full life. I also don't know how to deal with our internal hurts other than looking at them one at a time in a detached sorta way. But, maybe just identifying something as needing attention is a good start. No doubt, many people take unresolved traumas they received as a child to their grave. Here is where the animals can help if we let them. We "simply" need to clear space and have the intent of connecting with them. Let's do our part to create relationships with them where everyone wins. Personally, I think they spoil me. For a few dollars' worth of sugar, a hummer gave me the memory of feeling his little toenails on my finger. For a few bucks' worth of birdseed, I get to be up close to frolicking deer, slinking foxes, and rabbits playing chase…. and of course, lots and lots of birds!

The animals have helped teach me how to quiet my overactive mind and be present. They constantly give me the gift of interaction with them. They help me to see and deal with many of the pains that seem to be part of the human experience. In short, they spoil me! Oh, gotta go. The cat is becoming impatient! 😊

If an animal is hungry, feed that animal right now. Don't
wait.

Water Speaks

I sat down to write, and these
words flowed out—so like
Water...

You think you understand
me in so many ways, yet there
are extremely important ways in
which you don't know me at all. I
design and shape our world, yet
you only know the how of it. I give you life, but you understand only
some of the mechanics of being alive, and almost none of the why. You
treat me as a resource to be exploited and used up, just as you do with
nearly all of the world you live in, yet you don't seem to understand
that we are literally the foundation on which you stand, in every sense
of the word.

You are only capable of respecting that which you understand. So
it's time once again for you to understand me; if you don't, you will
suffer needlessly. Sailors who don't understand me are far more likely
to give me their lives, yet those who respect me can live to a serene old
age. Long ago, humanity had a much closer relationship with me and
the rest of the natural world. But now, for the most part, you've made
yourself too busy and preoccupied to really see or feel the life around
you. If you work to find quiet and take a far broader view than you are
accustomed to, you can begin to understand life and the part I play in it.

"To know me is to love me," is one of your sayings. You shall come
to know in your blood and your bones that I am an integral part of the
living universe, and that you are part of that same universe. When you
sit by a stream or an ocean, or sail around the world, or throw snowballs,

or simply enjoy your favorite drink, I bring you comfort. You and I are different facets of one living universe of love. Once you understand that there is no such thing as death, only change, you'll begin to understand and love the universe, me, and yourself beyond what you can presently imagine. This is so simple that it's hard to understand. Try to accept it.

Understand that life evolves and presents itself in many stages, energies, and forms. Some are easy for you to recognize, and others not so much. You seldom understand and see any life that is different from you. In your minds, things that move far more slowly or faster than you, cannot possibly be alive. You think life can only exist within a narrow temperature range, in your time frame, and under a blanket of air. Life is far, far grander than you imagine! Your ability to identify the physics that describe what something does doesn't mean you know what that thing is. Gravity and light are good examples of this, just as I am.

I have a long memory. Once I was stardust, just as you were. This planet coalesced from that dust, and eventually I formed into recognizable bodies of fluid, which you were born into. Your blood is much like the ancient seas. I have run in and around all of life here, and I remember and unite all of it. I am the connection on Earth for all of life, much like blood in your body connects every individual cell. And, much like the cells in your body, all of the "individuals" on Earth—whether human, insect, or tree—are part of the living web of life that you can easily recognize. The planet Herself exists in timeframes and has rhythms and energies that are sometimes too subtle and sometimes too big for you to perceive, yet that doesn't mean She isn't alive.

I tell you all of this to open your eyes and your heart to the incredible universe you are part of, so that you might grow respect for Her and understand that you have a role to play in helping all life live to its fullest potential, including your own.

Mama Cat's Diary

Transcriber's note: Mama Cat has not bothered to learn how to write, so I do it for her. These events began at a house I was fixing up in Salinas. Now Mama Cat tells the tale...

December 29: Human has put food out again. He's remarkably inconsistent about when he puts out food for me. Things are strange, though. This time, the food bowl is inside a wire box that has an open end. I sniff it quite a lot to make sure it's OK. Seems OK. I walk inside to have a nibble, and the end that was open closes. Trouble! Human is coming toward me. I lunge at the corners of the wire box, but it does not open. My paws are a bit bloody from the effort. Human picks up the box with me in it, then loads me into his noisy metal box on wheels and puts a towel over me. The box on wheels moves, and I hear strange sounds like wind, but higher-pitched. Finally, the box with wheels stops and Human picks me up in the wire box. He carries me into a bigger box that is light inside. He puts a small plastic box with a wire door and a handle up to the wire box I'm in (why do humans like boxes so much?). He moves to the end of the wire box, so of course I move away and into the plastic box. There is food and water in there, but I'm worried about what Human intends to do with me. I've heard a rumor that humans eat other animals for fun! He leaves me alone in a closed-off part of his bigger light box. Well, at least he didn't eat me right away. Hours later, he's back. I used to be free, and now I must tolerate this odor of Human. He just natters at me and then goes to sleep. I'm confused.

December 30: Human has trapped three of my children. I've not met true evil before. He parades them in front of me, and they act as if they don't

understand how dangerous he really is. My poor children; one is even scared of me! Human just let me out of the plastic box and into the bigger box he apparently calls a room. It has inadequate hiding places. I could touch my children now, but I don't dare; they appear to be on drugs, or maybe sick, and I can't risk catching what they have.

December 31: When I sit unmoving, I'm invisible. There are two places in this "room" where I sit. One is by a picture of the real world. Birds fly by and do not see me.

The other place where I sit is up high on a shelf where there are many small pieces of cloth that Human puts on his feet. Poor Human has no fur. Human leaves me alone much of the day, and I am safe to eat and drink. He did touch my back, in a stroking way, but I remained invisible, so it was OK. I'm experimenting with moving while Human is in the room. So far, so good. He seems to be unaware, and does not try to come eat me. His hearing must be defective.

January 1: It's minutes into the new day (by the human clock). I decide to have a drink and jump down from my place with the picture of the world. My child growls at me (Human calls him Watcher). I must bide my time until we can all escape and I can remind my children who they are.

I take a long drink. I try to get to my high-up place, but it's tricky with Human so close, and I slide off the wall. Might as well eat while I'm at ground level. It is strange, eating this unmoving crunchy brown stuff. Human is probably trying to fatten me up.

January 2: I don't understand Human. He natters at me and holds his paw out toward me. He keeps moving it closer, probably testing my nerves. He does not seem to understand that I'm invisible. He actually touched my invisible leg, nattered, and withdrew. Are they all so strange?

January 3: I am a very patient feline, but Human pesters me. Three times so far today, I've let him stroke my haunch. Training humans must be a challenge. If they grow up at all, it must be very slowly. I'm torn. Should I let him persist, or give him a good training bite? He offered me some foul-smelling protein in a small round box. I eat live animals, not long-dead ones. What's there to chase in a round box? Great Lion in the Sky, is this a test?

January 4: Despite my captivity, I'm feeling good tonight. I feel like roaming. For a while, I jump up to the picture of the real world, then back down, then back up. There is a half moon, so things are quite clear. My children stir, but do not take part. There is so much I want to share with them.

January 5: These days, Human seems to expect that he can just reach out and stroke my back and my haunch whenever he wishes. I let him do it, as there is probably little point in trying to train such a dim wit. He just came over to me and put both of his paws on me and simply left them for a while. Surprisingly, there was no pain. But he might have been salivating.

January 7: Silly Human! He tried his typical petting and leaving of paws on me. (This is when he's moving his paws around on me, making me pet him.) Then he tried to lift me off the ground! He only bled a little, and I didn't mean to damage him, but really! He's lucky I don't get upset easily. Being dense, he tried to lift me a second time, and for some unknown reason I let him. He put me into the little plastic-and-wire box and carried me out into a bigger version of the "room." My children were there. It was interesting for a while, looking around for the escape routes. Eventually, the human returned me to "my" room, opened the door to the little box, and left. I'm glad he showed me that small courtesy.

January 8: Well, he's back to putting his paws on me when I'm invisible, but now he gets petted, then lifts the covers to make me visible. Then he

lets the covers back down and gets
petted again. It might be my fault.
I prefer the tangle of soft cloth he
calls a bed. Human has a lot to
learn about etiquette. I suppose I
can tolerate petting his paws when
I'm invisible, but when he tries to expose me and stare directly at me
while reaching his paws towards me, that's just so rude—and threatening!
You only stare at your next meal! This is so obvious, but the human is
simple, and definitely not aware.

Aside from the human smell, it's warm and invisible under the covers;
nice. Problem is, he can reach me too easily. Well, as I seem to be locked
up in a loony bin, may as well play my part.

January 9: He grabbed me again and put me in the little box. I decided
not to kill him.

This time he took me around
and showed me different parts
of his big light box. I saw **lots** of
hiding places! After the tour, I got
under the covers but he reached
in, pulled me from my invisibility,
and set me on top of the tangle of cloth. At least I got a good look at my
children. He finally left, and I became invisible. After a time, it became
moon light and he was clearly asleep, so I came out and tried walking
on him. I traversed him from toe to shoulder, and he didn't even wake.
How strange it must be to sleep so deeply, as though you're nearly dead.
I walked on him more through the moonlit time. Silly Human must
imagine he's in charge. Let's keep it that way.

January 11: Perhaps it's a routine. I'm invisible under the covers, and
it's moon time. Human comes in and gets under the covers also. I wait
until he is incapacitated by sleep, and then slip out to roam the room.
I roam, I walk on Human, I talk to the Great Outdoors. Recently, I

tried getting invisible back under the warm cover even when Human is still there. Also, I don't put up much resistance when he lifts me off the ground, as he hasn't even nibbled on me yet. He tried putting me on top of his long leg-bones, where I sat patiently for nearly three seconds. Anyway, it seems I can move even though he must see me. He is a very strange predator.

January 13: Well, at least it's quiet. Human has been gone most of the time, and I sit quietly in this "room." It's good I don't get bored, or I'd have a bad case of it by now. I can hear my children running around in the bigger box, but it remains closed off to me.

When Human is here, I still pet his paws under the covers. He even uses his paws to rub behind my ears, which seems a curious thing to do to your meal. He tried putting me on his leg bones again, but I was having none of it and escaped. He also reached under the cover to get petted, but then he lifted the cover, so I was visible while he got petted. I suppose Human is using his pea brain to play mind games with me. I am a patient feline!

January 15: Yes, I am patient! I even petted the Human while I sat on the wooden shelf below the picture of the real world. He seems so needy of petting. He took me into the bigger light box, where I get to see how humans spend their time. I may sleep eighteen hours a day, but they are s-e-d-e-n-t-a-r-y! They just sit and look at flat things. At least my children seem to be healthy, if not brainwashed. Things are OK. I've now been here over half of the cycle of the Moon and have not yet been eaten.

January 24: Life remains unexciting most of the time, which is why I haven't written. There have been some interesting changes though. Human used to keep me closed up and alone when he wasn't here. Now he's keeping the partition between the "room" and the rest of the big box open. I go out at night and look around when Human is asleep. My child, the one Human calls Rex, even accompanies me. My child

is brainwashed. He likes Human and even trusts him. Must not fall into that trap!

February 1: The moon is growing. My children are also growing (physically, anyway). I continue to practice my invisibility, and clearly it's working; there are many times when Human cannot see me. He does break the spell at times and reaches under covers so that I pet his paws with my back and sometimes with my ears.

I'm free to wander around the bigger box at night, but the warmth of being under cover is good, even if my children occasionally walk on me and even if Human is too close. The exciting bits are what one would expect: Human tries to pick me up, Human tries to put me in a small cage, and Human violates all decency and stares directly at me. They are such slow learners!

February 11: Despite the threats, I'm now traveling in plain view of humans during the day. It really isn't so much of a risk; I'm about as likely to be caught and eaten by a rock. Also, when resting under the covers I can finally lie on my side. I run from humans, but for some reason they aren't so scary. One nice thing is there are so many places to be invisible. I keep finding different ones to try out. Now if they would only serve up some interesting food! I could go for a young finch right about now.

February 18: Human keeps coming after me. He needs petting. So today he reaches under the covers to get petted. I decided to make a break for it, but he'd closed the partition to the  bigger box. There I am, in the open, with human eyes on me. I blinked, he blinked. Strangely, Human held up the covers for me. I thought about it, and after showing Human about cat time, I walked directly past and under his paw to go under the covers. Of course, needy Human spoiled things by reaching in to get more petting.

On the plus side, humans make good latrine cleaners, when they remember.

February 22: I suppose I've fallen into a routine. Also, getting Human to take the necessary dictation has been difficult. I get up when Human goes to bed. I often rest with my children in the bigger part of the light box, both during the day and in dark times.

Of course, I keep my distance from humans, but it isn't a firm rule. I even let Human get petted in the open. Once. He does continue to reach under covers for more petting, and now I have no real trouble with it. He's obviously needy, and I'm patient. My children purr around Human. Petting him does indeed feel nice, but I have not sunk so low as to purr.

June 29: It's pleasant when Human is gone. Things are quieter, there is less 'eau de human,' and, most importantly, he's not trying to get petted by my haunch and my ears when he isn't here. I also get to lounge with my  children, largely unseen. But now Human is back and trying to sneak up on me again. I did let him rest his paw on me while I was in the open. I even let his paw get petted while I was being bathed by my child; I pretended not to notice. My ability to tolerate him has increased. He can place his mitt within four inches before I feel the urge to tilt away. But I'm not really sure if this is a good or a bad thing.

July 6: Should I be embarrassed? My children were playing with the little round sparkly noisy ball that Human gave them. Must have let my guard down, because I found myself—descendant of Great Lion!—playing with it too. I only did it for a short span of time. Human probably didn't even notice. Rodents are certainly more entertaining, but this was better than nothing. If Human was intelligent, he'd bring some rodents into this big light box for us to hunt. A finch would be nice too...Well, a cat can dream.

July 14: It was a strange event. I had forgotten I could do it, or maybe I never knew how. Of course, all things strange involve Human somehow. My children were petting him while I was under the covers. They were very  close by, and they were purring. Human reached under the cover, as he does, and was petted as I often permit him to be. I assumed the purring came from my brainwashed children, but was surprised to find it coming from me! Yes, petting him does feel nice, but—really! It must be some hormonal imbalance. What else could account for it? Human must have noticed how much we enjoy bathing each other, and petting has some similarity. Hmmmmm.

August 20: I must be going soft. Needy Human is finally figuring out that it's his paws I'm wary of, so he's putting his largely hairless face right up to mine these days. I don't mind, aside from the breath. I can stay relaxed even with him breathing on me, only inches away. When he lifts up his mitts and gets too close with them, I remind him of the rules. He might be learning, though that's a lot to hope for.

There is a new soft place that has sun warmth, where I can actually relax. I even had some of that protein out of the round  box and thought it was OK. I'm definitely going soft.

September 1: Well, I've now been trapped here for over five years (cat time), and no physical damage has come to me aside from a slightly rounder midsection. Is it possible that I was wrong about Human? The real likelihood is that he's even more twisted than I care to imagine. Still, I'm figuring out how to relax amongst monsters. Human breathes on me and I'm unperturbed. He waits until I'm sleepy and plays with my toes. I pretend to be asleep. He sticks his little flat talking box into my face and it flashes. I only blink. As Winston Catchill said generations ago, "If you're going through hell, keep going."

September 23: It's a day like any other. Human did go around and spray smelly stuff on the pictures of the real world and then rub them. I suppose he just likes rubbing things, including me, though my eyes seem to be a bit sharper when I'm looking at the real world now. I was resting

in my invisibility, and Human came by to get petted. I allowed a little purr to come out, as he is so, so needy. He then slowly lifted my invisibility over the span of many petting strokes. Finally, Human stopped getting petted and left me largely visible. He backed away and stared into his little flat thing that flashes at me sometimes.

What a strange turn of events this life has taken! Stranger still is that I have adapted to it. Cohabitating with humans… who would have thought?

Housing

Dreaming About Housing

There is a lot about how we design and build homes that could use a little rethinking. Housing should be affordable, effective and efficient. These days, broadly speaking, it doesn't do any of those jobs well. I'd like to tackle some of  the bigger hurdles which are interfering with the implied promise of housing, which is to provide a safe, comfortable, and adaptable space for us to live life well and affordably.

I'm a general contractor, and my brother and my uncle are both architects. I've spent many years dealing with homes in need. As a result, I've been exposed to what's out there in the built world, both good and not so much, and I've gotten to peer into our culture-wide thinking about what homes should provide for their occupants. So much of how we build homes is driven by tradition. Our predecessors developed most of their norms and practices when the building landscape was vastly different than it is now. A good example of this is that we build homes on site, one board at a time. It's called stick building. But think about how much better it could be if homes were built in factories and delivered to the job site in large pieces that could then be fastened together. I once saw a video of what it would look like to build a car in the middle of a muddy field versus building it on a production line in a factory. That video drove home the point that houses would be far better off being built under controlled conditions, where templates and jigs were all set up for accomplishing precision work in a dry, flat, clean environment. This approach can save months of time, many dollars and much messiness.

Sadly, there are architects out there who design for magazine covers. This means that they are doing showy work with the hope of gaining some celebrity status. That's all fine, but it might mean they aren't really focused on their clients' needs. This reinforces the notion that if you plan on building a house, you need to do your homework and have a very good idea of what you want and how an architect can help you reach those goals.

An example of a way in which homes could be built to better take care of their occupants' needs would be to design them in response to the natural surroundings, like we used to do. Where does the sun rise and set? What are the prevailing winds? When might cooling be needed and how might it be accomplished? Understanding things like these allows the building to be more comfortable and energy efficient at the same time. An example of this is appropriately placed roof overhangs to keep the hot sun out instead of using air conditioning. This is precisely where your architect should be able to help you work through the available choices.

Then there are building contractors who compete to get the job by having the lowest bid. This forces them to leave little margin for error or change, so they work fast and cheap, cutting any corners they can. Don't forget that building to code is a minimum standard. Bragging that you build to code is like saying proudly that you do D- work. Low first cost is nice, but low life-cycle cost is far nicer! Insulation gives us a great example to consider. Insulating to code will give you a home that's reasonably efficient today, but what about twenty years from now? Energy costs just go up. Building codes have consistently required more insulation. So why not overdo the level of insulation so it is still cost effective twenty years from now, even when energy costs have doubled? Adding more insulation is usually a very difficult thing to do in an existing home, so we generally don't fix it, but instead suffer with higher utility bills and less comfort. Let's rethink the low bidder approach and shop for housing based on life-cycle cost.

Then there are the owners; they want a good job done, but they aren't educated in the nuances of getting a building built and they don't even know what questions to ask. Unhappy surprises may result. So many times, I've heard stories of homeowners who left town for the big building or remodeling process to happen and then were dismayed at how different the result was from their expectations. It would be incredibly useful if the local junior college offered a class to prospective home-owners/builders on what the process of building a home entails, and how to best navigate it. Money could be saved, and grey hair avoided.

I haven't even mentioned the planning and building departments, where rules seem to be created on a whim, change often, are seldom explained well, and sometimes aren't enforced evenly. Some building inspectors act like demigods, seemingly interpreting building codes according to their mood at the moment.

With each category above, there are the good exceptions wherein professionals actually act professionally and are helpful. But that is certainly, and sadly, not the rule.

Throw all these competing and conflicting interests together, and it's no wonder that building is usually one of the most stressful and expensive experiences a homeowner ever goes through.

There are ways to avoid much of the custom home mess described above. Two of my favorite ways are to remodel a run-down house, or to install a manufactured home.

If you live in an area where building departments are notoriously difficult to deal with, remodeling may be easier than starting from scratch. This could mean anything from adding a room or redoing a kitchen to buying a really run-down house and doing a major remodel, sometimes called a "gut rehab" because it starts with gutting the house and ripping out everything down to the framing. (I've heard of owners who tore out everything but the front door, so the word "remodel" is sort of a joke in some cases.)

Another approach is to go with manufactured housing. This puts the construction under federal guidelines and removes much of it from the jurisdiction of local authorities. If you want a manufactured home, it's important to really do your shopping. Manufactured housing sometimes suffers from cost-cutting, or "cheapifying," in a big way. Also, manufactured housing is looked down on by many in the trades because of that cheap reputation and usually lower resale value than standard stick-built housing. Then again, there are many high-end pre-fabricated home companies. You want something that will hold up and perform well for many decades, if not hundreds of years, and that will take some exploration to discover. I chose a middle ground in building my house—somewhere between on-site construction and off-site manufacturing. I used SIPs, which stands for structural insulated panel system. You give the SIP manufacturer your house plans, and they cut panels for you to assemble. You pour your foundation, then assemble the pre-made panels on site. It's a far faster and more precise way to build than stick-framing, and you get a much more energy-efficient shell for the house. In my experience, although the materials cost a little more, the savings in labor costs mean that you get a better home for no more money than you would have spent in a traditional build. As I did much of the labor on my home, my costs were far below the going rate for new construction at the time: my house cost about $100 per square foot, versus an average of $250 per foot for site-framed construction. Not bad savings! Also, I used far more insulation than was thought to be sane at the time. That insulation allowed me to put in a tiny heating system, and now nobody is telling me how silly my thick insulation is.

There are other opportunities to consider when building a home—things that often get overlooked, mostly because of tradition and habit. We commonly build homes with crawl spaces and attics. These are wonderful places for rodents and bugs to live, and great opportunities to lose energy in various ways. They are useless as living space, which is what people build homes for. We build these spaces anyway so that there are places to put mechanical systems and plumbing, but with a little thought, we can do better!

If, instead of building a wood-framed floor over a crawl space, we make the ground floor an insulated concrete slab, that concrete becomes thermal mass for the house, keeping temperatures more even. Plumbing pipes and electrical wiring that must go under the concrete may be put in conduit, so they're protected from damp soil and are easier to replace if needed. If a hydronic system is used for heating or even cooling, the need for an attic full of ductwork goes away! A 1/2" water line can carry as many BTUs as a 7" air duct. It's a lot easier to fit a small water line into a building, and if the heating/cooling loads are kept low (by having a snug, well-insulated shell), you won't even need much of that small water line. So, if the shell of the house is well-insulated and airtight. then the heating and cooling loads will be far smaller and simpler to meet with much less equipment. You'll save money on both construction and operation.

The purpose of a home isn't to ignore and disconnect us from the environment surrounding us. Done well, it should help us reconnect, but most modern homes are oriented to make it easier for the car to come and go, rather than for the people to easily relate to and benefit from their surroundings.

My point is that, by thinking a bit differently, we can get greater benefits from our homes, and at a lower cost both financially and emotionally. Would you rather have an OK place to live, or a wonderful home to live in? It really is your choice!

 Ask yourself what can go right. It balances what can go wrong.

REALLY Low-Cost Homes

I've been thinking about housing much of my life. Simply put, one of the big problems with housing is that most people in the U.S. cannot afford to own it. In school, we are not taught much that's useful about how to manage money or how to think about it, so the majority of us have little stashed away for emergencies or retirement, and cannot come up with even the down payment on a conventional home. That's sad, as it makes us slaves to our lack of money. For most folks, a home is the biggest investment—or indebtedness—they will ever take on. That's a good reason to understand more about how both money and real estate work. We never want to invest in something we don't understand very well!

So, I've been pondering how to "do" housing in a way that costs far less, yet still meets our needs. We have lots of expectations around housing, but to drastically reduce the cost of it we'll need to adjust some of those expectations. The "standard" expectation is to have a nice stick-built home, on a nice lot, in a nice part of town. But I want to suggest that if we change our expectations, many more people can not only own their home, but enjoy the benefits of living in community. My proposal is to have some sort of manufactured housing in a small development. There are many other ways to cut the cost of housing, but this way has so many benefits, I thought I'd start with it. The recent interest in smaller homes might be moving us in this direction. The concept I'd like to bring up is called cohousing.

The normal approach of owning an independent lot, bringing utilities to it, and building a single house on it isn't cheap. How about changing things up a little and following the cohousing model to create community and spread the costs of land development and construction among the community members? Cohousing is briefly defined as "semi-communal housing consisting of a cluster of private homes and a shared community space (as for cooking or laundry facilities)." There are some resources at the end of this essay that can help you to better understand cohousing.

Or let's imagine a hybrid of a trailer park and cohousing. Following cohousing guidelines, the park would be people-centric rather than car-centric. It would have a main building that housed a kitchen, room for gatherings, laundry facilities, maybe a shop, and even some guest bedrooms. That building would get a lot of use and would minimize the need for those functions in the private homes—which could then be even simpler and smaller (read less expensive!). The homes themselves could be secondhand mobile homes or RVs, and therefore much less expensive than new construction.

A good cohousing development includes up to thirty-five homes; splitting infrastructure costs thirty-five ways helps cut the individual cost of developing the land. So, buying into a development like this could cost far less than purchasing a normal single-family home. Also, you'd have a community in which people get to know and care for each other, making life safer and more enjoyable. Finally, when a cohousing community is built, property values around it usually go up, so neighbors are happy, too.

But there are even more benefits to adopting the cohousing model. The community could choose to have shared outdoor spaces, such as a big vegetable garden and a playground. Residents could teach classes based on their skills, and shared responsibilities like child-sitting or elder-care could be woven into the fabric of life. These things all add up to the potential for a richer life than the usual semi-isolated single-family home can give.

I just did a search on craigslist for Recreational Vehicles (RVs) in Northern California, at a maximum asking price of $10,000. There were lots of them! I imagine it will be pretty much the same across the country. Certainly, many of these RVs will need work, but even if fixing them up doubles the cost, things could be worse.

Mobile homes are another place to look for affordable housing. It's not uncommon that people who own mobile homes in parks fail to pay their space rent for any number of reasons. One common reason is that they up and die and no relatives can be found, or the relatives have no interest in the mobile home. These homes can sometimes be had for free or just for the unpaid space rent. Another common way to get an inexpensive mobile home is when someone sells a piece of land with a mobile home on it, but the buyer just wants the home moved off the property. These homes will be cheap or free. The costs of ownership are in having a place to move the home to, and then moving it.

If you step back and think about it, these two types of dwellings (RVs and mobile homes) are the small and tiny homes of yesteryear. But think about the cost. You can buy an RV for roughly $40 or less per square foot, in great shape. It's not hard to find older, livable mobile homes for $10 per square foot. But a new tiny home can often cost over $500 per square foot.

If the "tiny home" idea sounds too tight for comfort, there are ways to create indoor/outdoor spaces that bring the benefits of nature inside and give you more real living space that changes with the seasons. It's a fun and interesting approach that blurs the line between inside and outside, extending your living area inexpensively. An additional benefit is that if you don't like the look of an RV or mobile home, adding outdoor spaces can just about make those made-in-a-factory-looking walls disappear.

Unfortunately, many of the biggest hurdles to overcoming expensive housing are baked into our regulations and how they are enforced. Many municipalities discourage manufactured housing of all sorts because they think it's substandard or will bring adjacent property values down—or will not yield as much property tax as conventional construction! Still, public officials decry our lack of affordable housing. Perhaps they need to encourage, rather than put up barriers to, novel thinking about low-cost housing, so that we can test and learn what works in the real world.

AARP wrote interesting primer on cohousing. Look for Cohousing: A Growing Concept in Communal Living. For a **lot** more information look for the Cohousing Community.

How to Look at a House

That's a pretty silly title, isn't it? Well, you look at a house and you see, um, a house. It may be a pretty one or a beat-up one; it may have awful colors or chipped paint. But what is there to really see? It all depends on your perspective. Perspective affects how we see things, and thereby influences what we actually do see.

Notice the sagging roof, boarded up windows, and deteriorated roofing? This place might not have good bones!

For the purposes of this discussion, we're looking at the house as an investment—not a "lipstick flipper" sort of investment, in which you do cosmetic repairs only, but an investment in the sorts of repairs and upgrades that would make the home safe, durable, efficient, and a pleasure to live in. If you're investing for profit, the planning also needs to include your "exit strategy"—i.e., rent out or sell—and your desire not to lose money.

So, how does this contractor look at a home? I'm looking for a house that has "good bones," and I start from the street. Look at the roof line: Is there any sagging? Are the walls actually vertical? If things are crooked, you know it will take a lot of structural work to straighten things out. A crooked house may need foundation work, termite work, or both. Or maybe the house was built before there were building codes and doesn't even have stud walls or a concrete foundation. A house with "good bones" is straight and true, is made with adequate materials, has a good foundation, and shows no extensive rot or bug problems. Plumbing, insulation, windows, electrical systems, and heating and cooling systems can all be fixed or upgraded, but they don't really affect the bones of a house. If the bones are bad, the home will probably cost too much to fix; it can't be a good investment.

That said, I look for homes that scare other investors off. I need to see through the bad stuff to know if the bones are decent. For example, graffiti tends to scare others off. To me, it just means the house needs to be made secure and that graffiti needs to be painted over. Homes are often piled high with trash, and people find this off-putting. I see the trash and think about how many dump runs it means. I also think about how happy the neighbors will be when that trash is gone.

Scary homes often have appealing prices. If you're a wannabe homeowner with some fix-it skills, look for scary houses in nice neighborhoods. With housing prices these days, this could be a very good way to sidestep the crazy prices and still get your home sweet home. There is no law that says only investors can buy scary homes!

The next thing I do when looking at a house is to get inside and look up. Are there water marks on the ceiling? Has the ceiling fallen in? Water is a home's single biggest enemy. It can cause rot, invite bugs, undermine the foundation, and create a perfect place for mold to grow. If you want to know a lot more about water and buildings, visit www.buildingscience.com. It's a big topic! But if we walked into the building and found good bones and no real water damage, that's great.

Next, I look into the attic and crawl space or basement, if there is one, and see what's there. These are places where the mechanical bits of a home live—ductwork, wiring, and plumbing. Crawling around under a house is sort of a time-bender; you'll see evidence of leaks that may have been fixed decades ago…or not at all. You may see old generations of plumbing that weren't removed when new plumbing was installed. You'll get a feel for how many different hands have worked on the place and how skilled or unskilled those hands were! Also, you get to look around for evidence of bugs. You may see termite tunnels coming up the foundation wall, or piles of frass (poop) the termites left behind. It's essential to know what you're dealing with. The internet has plenty of images of termite tunnels and frass for your viewing pleasure!

Then I go back outside to look at the roofing material and get an idea of how much life it has left. Installing a new roof is usually the single biggest repair cost in renovating a home—often a five-figure item. Composition roofing shingles are far and away the most common type.

If there are gutters on a comp shingle roof, I'll have a look in them for that fine gravel that washes off the roofing. If there's a lot, that suggests the composition roofing is getting old. I also look for broken tabs and exposed felt in the shingles, evidence of repairs, and rotted rafter tails.

There is a lot more that could be said about inspecting a home, but having good bones—meaning a solid frame to work from—is the most important thing. If this isn't something you know how to do, hire an experienced contractor to tour the house with you and take notes. You'll learn as you go!

 Long-term, there is no good point in doing a job half-way.

Lessons in Power from Off the Grid

Back in 2006, I finished building my off-grid home. I had a lot of ideas to try out, so I got to experiment on my own home in ways you wouldn't want to do for, or to, another person. I was my own guinea pig. Following are some lists of things I learned along the way. Rules seem to be for bending sometimes, so I did—and mostly it worked out.

Using Less Electricity

Get rid of electrical standby losses

- Attempt to use no "wall warts." These are the little plug-in transformers that sip power all the time.

- Minimize power draw from GFI (ground fault interrupter) outlets. (GFI circuit breakers can use 1/4 the energy of GFI outlets, so rather than use sixteen GFI outlets, I used three GFI breakers and two switch-controlled GFI outlets, similar to what they do in Great Britain.)

- Put electronics, such as the computer, and any necessary wall warts on power strips. (Note that some power strips have their own electronics and standby losses!) Of course, turn off the power strips when not being used.

- Don't trust name-tag electricity-usage ratings. Use a Kill-a-Watt or similar meter to actually know power draw and usage.

- Use little resistance heating or electric motors.

- Insulate and seal the house shell or envelope well, so that you only need small, non-electric heating/cooling systems.

- Consider using an old-fashioned water-based, gravity-driven heating system. These were common before houses were electrified.

- Use mechanical thermostatic controls, rather than electrical. Wax driven cylinders, such as those used in greenhouses, can work nicely.

- Use a well-insulated, chest-style freezer as a fridge. This well-insulated box won't let all the cold air fall out when you open the door. It's not difficult to add plug in thermostatic controls to make this conversion.

Cut down on electrical use for lighting

- Use an open house design to allow light to bounce around the interior.

- Paint ceilings bright white to better bounce light around.

- Cut holes in walls (insert translucent plastic if needed for privacy or concerns about air movement) to allow light to go where it's wanted.

- Use LEDs; they have come a long way and can now effectively replace nearly all other forms of lighting.

- Size your circuit breakers one size down for the wiring it serves. An example would be to use a fifteen-amp breaker for twelve-gauge copper wire instead of fourteen-gauge wire. This greatly reduces the possibility of line losses.

Think like an Off-Gridder (some things to keep in mind when aiming for efficiency)

- Reducing loads and using power efficiently allowed me to build a much smaller, less expensive photovoltaic (PV, or solar electric) system. Power electronics that need to always be on, such as a portable phone or answering machine, via a small inverter that has a far smaller power draw than the large inverter that powers the rest of the house.

- My house draws less than fifteen watts of standby power. This keeps the main inverter in sleep mode, saving quite a bit of energy. (Note that inverter technology keeps changing, so get current inverter specs to find out what you really need.)

- The lighting is primarily twenty-four volts DC. This prevents the need to wake up the main inverter, (which draws fifty-five-watts just to be awake), for small loads. I installed a separate twenty-four volt DC system in the house for lighting and many outlets.

- The house was originally powered by 630 watts of PV. After adding electric refrigeration, I had to increase the size of the PV system to 890 watts. Now I've decided to completely get rid of propane. This means induction cooking and a heat pump water heater. I expanded my PV system again, up to 1500 watts, which is still considered to be a small system. This is where you can really see the cost-effectiveness of energy efficiency. My system is roughly 1/4 the size and cost of a system for a "built to code" house of the same size.

Breaking the Rules (Questioning dogma)

- In northern latitudes, solar-heated homes must face south. My house faces north. Basically, if your house has large windows facing the sun, you are living inside a solar collector. It's going to get hot and cold! Keeping much of the sun out of the house makes it far easier to control those temperature swings. A big, south-facing roof provides the ideal place for solar collectors, too.

- Build thermal mass into the house to take advantage of direct solar gain. Normally, thermal mass is cement, which soaks up heat and then slowly releases it when things cool down. The thermal mass in this house, which is water, moves around the house as needed to keep the spaces comfortable. By the way, pound for pound, water holds about six times as much heat as cement does. Fixed mass would cost a lot more, and could leave spaces cold in winter without direct solar gain.

- For solar water-heating, you need one to one and a half gallons of water per square foot of solar collector. In this house, six, thirty-two-square-foot solar-thermal collectors heat the "thermal mass," which is 1,000 gallons of water. This works out to over five gallons of water per square foot of collector. It allows low-grade heat to be collected and used over more days per year. The house can be kept at seventy degrees, via eighty-degree water.

- Solar thermal cannot economically be used to heat a house. "Solar thermal" refers to heating either water (or another fluid) or air. These then give up their heat to the house to keep it comfortable. If the home is well insulated, with little unintentional air leakage, solar thermal can work nicely for space heating most of the year. Even so, 100 percent solar heating is impractical for many homes. Some sort of backup heating is necessary. I have a backup wood stove and use about 1/4 cord of wood per year.

- It costs more to build a solar-powered house. By doing much of the work myself, and by shopping carefully, this house cost about $100 per square foot, as opposed to the norm in this area of $250. If you're not going to do the work yourself, it's crucial that you design for cost-efficiency and find talented tradespeople who can listen to what you want.

- It's important to follow guidelines set out by others to ensure that you do the right thing. It's more important to build something you want than to build your home to satisfy others' rules or the next owner's anticipated needs. The basic principles I worked for in this house were quiet, low upkeep, high energy-efficiency, comfort, and affordability. "Quiet," for example, is not important in any guidelines I've seen, yet guests often remark on how nice the quiet is.

Indoor Air Quality

- Tight construction means reduced utility bills, but also threatens air quality. So, I took several measures to minimize threats to indoor air quality.

- The first plumbing in this house was a central vacuum cleaner, made from ABS pipe and a shop vac. It vents to the outside, so once dust is picked up, it's really gone.

- The water heater is direct-vent (as was the original gas fridge), to send combustion byproducts straight outdoors.

- The wood stove takes combustion air from outside the living space.

- The kitchen stove fumes are removed via an exhaust fan that has an integral airtight door.

- I switched from a gas stove to induction cooking. This eliminates pollutants from burning gas inside the house.

- The house is three stories tall, so the "stack" or chimney effect allows good natural ventilation by just opening windows.

- I used low-VOC (volatile organic compound) building materials where possible, but they weren't always available at the time. Hence, early in the life of the house, I needed to seal what could be sealed (like painting the indoor oriented strand board, and then ventilate more than normal, to allow the materials to off-gas).

Creative Heating Systems for Energy-Efficient Homes

- The house gets water from a deep well, which normally would require a lot of pumping power. Instead, I used a positive-displacement pump to move water to an uphill tank for gravity-supply to the house. As this is powered from the house's system, any water waste creates an unnecessary electrical cost. Saving water saves electricity.

- This house has a calculated heat loss of 27,000 BTU/hr. Most forced-air heating equipment is sized for much bigger loads.

- A water-based heating system saves space in the house and can move heat around far more efficiently than by using air. Dirty ducts and duct leakage concerns disappear.

- My house uses radiant heating tubes in the walls, rather than in the floor. This allowed me to build a no-pump system, because gravity moves the water (as the water cools, it becomes denser and sinks downward). It also doesn't place limitations on floor coverings or temperature, as floor-based hydronic systems do. Additionally, the warm fin-tube is placed in the walls near windows and doors—areas with the greatest heat loss. This way, heat is balanced for a more comfortable house.

This Plumbing Isn't Like Your Grandfather's

- Modern plumbing fixtures use less water than our ancestors' fixtures did, but plumbing codes aren't keeping up. Codes would make you oversize piping, creating water and energy waste.

- My house uses a 3/8" PEX manifold system to deliver hot and cold water. The hot manifold is placed on top of the water heater, so hot water floats up into it, keeping it full of hot water. This ultimately means faster hot water at the tap.

- 3/8" tubing contains half the water that half inch tubing does, so with adequate pressure, the wait time and water/energy waste is cut in half.

- PEX is a good material for both new construction and retrofits, as it's relatively easy to run through structures.

- I chose a manifold system (which is basically a number of small outlets on a single bigger pipe), as it needs no pump. Another alternative is to place small manifolds around the house, close to places like the kitchen and bathrooms. Then use a pump to move hot water into the lines when you want hot water. This approach works nicely, particularly where fixtures are spread out.

- A shower heat-exchanger is in place under the main shower. It captures 60 percent of the heat that would otherwise be lost down the drain.

- Drain lines are a maximum of three inches in diameter. With low-flow toilets, bigger lines tend to clog up as the lines are not rinsed well by the available water. Fixture water usage will continue to decrease, making properly sized water and waste lines more important.

Looking Ahead

- No matter how nice the design of an energy-efficient house, it can really only be efficient if it's used thoughtfully. Homeowner education and quick feedback from building systems will allow that possibility. There was a learning curve for living comfortably in my house, but once learned, it has been simple to manage.

- I've listed a bunch of (mostly) little things that can be done to make any home far more energy efficient and comfortable. Individually they aren't big, but cumulatively they could give you the option of being off grid if you want. At a minimum, being super-efficient lets you coast through power outages that would have others scrambling for a motel. In a best-case scenario, with your own power system, you aren't affected at all when the grid is down—and there is some satisfaction in that!

 Perspective is one of the most powerful tools you can have.

Systems Thinking Applied to Buildings

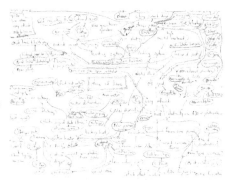

All modern buildings are made up of many different systems, all put together somehow. When they're put together well, the results can be wonderful, combining comfort in various forms: good temperature, proper humidity, low noise, appropriate light, very low pollutant levels, and an easy-to-live-with cost. Certainly, there are other comforts, too, such as long building life and low maintenance.

In order to put all these parts together well, systems thinking should be integral to the design and construction processes. Systems thinking is a process of vetting ideas through multiple perspectives: How will your work affect other trades or building systems? How will it last and perform over time? Can it be modified if need be? Should we design for today's energy costs, or for those costs twenty years from now, or for the life of the building? How will the environment the building lives in change with time, and how can we design for that now?

Mind mapping is a great tool for organizing complex projects. The image that goes with this chapter is the mind map I drew when designing my house. A mind map is a graphic outline that allows you to capture every relevant thing that comes to mind along with how it relates to other parts of the picture. It's amazingly helpful for practicing systems thinking. There are a number of mind-mapping tools online.

For my house, I had a short list of main goals, which you will see in the upper left-hand corner of my mind map. I wanted the house to be:

- quiet
- low-upkeep

- very energy-efficient
- easy to live in affordably

Never forgetting those goals during design and construction—and being able to easily see how they tied in with many other aspects of the project via the mind map—made them fairly easy to reach.

I've been on construction sites where the "systems thinking" concept didn't get thought about much. It's a classic situation: the framer puts up the walls and roof, then the plumber or electrician comes and bores big holes through the framing that weaken the structure. Or the plumber comes along first, then the framer has to figure out how to put the wood in the proper places.

Linda Wigington, founder of the Affordable Comfort Conference (now the National Home Performance Conference), has made it part of her mission to apply systems thinking to buildings and help others to understand the value of doing so. Integral to her thinking is the fact that each part of a building affects other parts: a good, snug building shell reduces the size and power of the equipment needed for heating and cooling; putting in less south-facing glass reduces cooling needs and room overheating; installing "way too much" insulation provides greater comfort right away via lower utility bills and more even temperatures along with future-proofing the building against rising energy costs.

I deal a lot with hot water. On the face of it, installing a low-flow shower head is a good thing, right? It should save water and energy, but let's look at what really happens. If you could find a shower head that gave you exactly half as much water as a conventional (2.5 gallons per minute) head, and did nothing with the piping serving that head, it should take twice as long to get hot water because the volume of water in the line hasn't changed. So, if it used to take one minute, now it will take two. Actually, it gets a bit worse. Because hot water is spending more time in the line, it will lose more heat and make you wait even longer for that hot water to arrive at the shower head. But if you approach the issue as a whole system, you'll supply those low-flow fixtures with low-volume plumbing. If you can replace the old 1/2" lines with 3/8" PEX piping, you'll cut the volume of water in the line in half. Then you don't have to waste as much water or wait so long for the shower to be useful! With hot water, it's clear that one will be better served by looking at all the parts of the system together.

It works the same way for the whole building. Buildings work best if they're designed to relate to factors in the environment where they're built, such as the sun's path, prevailing winds, groundwater level, ambient noise, and so forth.

Then there's the people part of systems thinking. We have to think about how to build the building so that there are no conflicts among the trades. We also want the owner, builder, and architect to be aligned in their goals so that conflict among them doesn't happen, either. Oh, and it would be nice if it satisfies the needs and wants of the new owners, too!

Building from scratch is a big, multi-faceted endeavor, and something that shouldn't be rushed. When I built my own home, it frustrated me that it took eight years just to get a building permit. But the upside to that delay was that I got to think through the many parts of the job in detail and really understand how they all fit together. This resulted in almost no changes being made during construction, which is rare, and saved building time and money.

To sum up, everything affects everything else in a building. It's sometimes not too easy to see the interrelationships, but you'll be better off assuming they exist and doing what you can to help all the parts and people get along harmoniously.

On Making a Cat Happy...
and Other Worthwhile Purr-suits

Petting a cat (done well) is of great value to both cat and person. Yet an outside observer may not see any benefit, so it seems like a waste of time. Activities like cat-petting don't directly benefit those not involved. A very old question—"What's in it for me?"—might help shed some light on the problem. That question is always useful if you want to get quickly to a perspective others may have. It places you firmly in their shoes.

So, it may be boring or even nice to see a cat being petted. It's nicer if you already know either the cat or the person doing the petting. It's better yet if you know both. But it really hits home if you are the one doing the petting, getting that cat to smile! Clearly, not petting the cat is unproductive—a waste of time!

How is it that petting a cat is so good for the human? It's all about making a connection. If you just stroke a cat's back as you walk by on your way to other tasks, that's nice, but it's not all that satisfying for either party. If you quiet your mind, focus on the cat, and let the cat give you clues about what feels good, the experience is very different! (By the way, I'm not excluding dogs or others here. Dogs are usually far easier to read than cats, so knowing what they want is often not tricky.)

A cat who lives with me, Shadow, has been around since I bottle-fed him as a little kitten. He's about ten now, so he's had time to teach me a thing or two. When he's thirsty, he sits by the bathroom door and looks up at the sink. That's a clue to pick him up, put him on the counter, and make a trickle run from the faucet. It must be just the right trickle, and I need to pet him just so while he considers the suitability of that trickle. This warms him up for the lapping to come. Next, it's my job to stick around and appreciate his lapping technique. Mess up any one part of the sequence, and he just jumps off and wanders away. Done right, however, he gets water running off his nose so that he can lap it up in the proper manner.

Shadow's brother, Rex, used to put his paw in the stream of water and lap from there. Everyone is different. Of course, Shadow can just go to the water dish and drink, but that's mere subsistence. Having water delivered to you in just the right manner by your adoring human is a lot more fun! Shadow and his brethren have much to teach the humans about how to truly be in the moment and live life fully. Luckily for us, they are patient and dedicated to the task of helping us grow up and become.

Another worthwhile pursuit for humans is to actually, really, and truly see the world around us. It's very hard to do this when our minds are full of noise and we're zooming around all over town. Many of us have so many plates spinning—and they all need to be kept revved up—that it's hard to find time to just be still and take in the magnificent world in and around us. The spinning plates certainly come from how we were taught to live and from societal pressures. Also, we put pressure on ourselves to do the most, be the best, or compete the hardest. Our success is usually measured in dollars rather than in satisfaction with life.

One way of dealing with all of this is simply to ask some questions: What's true? What's important? What feels satisfying right now? Questions like these help us filter out the less important or less useful stuff, letting us simplify and focus on what actually matters.

Have you ever simply sat quietly and watched the many phases a sunset can go through? Every minute presents a different face to enjoy. And there are so many rhythms in this world to take notice of! Think about the phases of the moon, the arc of sun, the seasons, and animal behaviors. Then the plant kingdom has its own rhythms. We're surrounded by, and part of, a rhythmic symphony!

Tuning in to the phases and pace of the world can quiet the internal noise, slow the frenetic speed, and provide clarity of vision and purpose. I love to watch the good ideas that fall into my mind when I quiet the noise and remove the clutter. Having that little bit of free space seems to make room for those good ideas to appear, and that makes both me and the cat happy.

Realities

Mom Taught by Example

My Mom taught me **lots** of things, but seldom was it just with words. She was an art major in school, so she taught me an appreciation of art by doing it. She worked in multiple media, including woodcarving, oil paint, clay, even making things of carved foam, covered with gesso and painted. My first scar came from trying out wood carving at five years old. That's when I learned to cut a-w-a-y from myself!

Her self-portrait, which you see here, is always watching me as I walk by! Her expression even changes just a bit, depending on whether she's sharing my happiness, or concerned, or just feeling contented. To me, there is a life in the painting that remains vibrant and present. Mom has only left physically.

Growing up, Mom learned a flexible strength that served her well for the rest of her life. In grade school, one challenge was that she got tall fast, so she was a head above even the guys; she felt awkward until they all caught up, just because she was different. Another strength-building moment was that her father died young, right in front of her at the dining table. The bonds among her and my grandmother and grand aunts grew stronger because of that moment. Her college roommate told me of visiting my mom's family home, and how the love in the air was palpable. This clearly was the antidote for loss and pain rather than sinking into depression or fear.

Mom taught me the importance of giving and being of service. She was the president of the local Woman's Democratic Club for sixteen years; helped found The Lyceum, which teaches gifted students while challenging them along the way; and a volunteer with the Red Cross. She helped create and develop our local hospital, helped start the local art museum, and for over twenty-five years spent eleven months of every year making Christmas tree ornaments to benefit that museum. I have no idea how she fit all that in along with raising four sons, but she did.

When I was a kid, Mom encouraged me to be whatever I wanted to be. For example, I loved to climb pine trees. When she saw me sixty to seventy feet up a pine, she'd just say, "I can't watch," and go back inside. I never got scolded for stuff like that, but learned self-reliance instead. She encouraged me to be who I wanted to be. She'd sit me down and ask what I wanted to do. I told her once that I wanted to be an inventor and create useful things. She didn't say that I should get a real job first. She encouraged me to invent by noticing problems and then creating their solutions. I began back then to see what was difficult for people and come up with solutions. It's fun to see the world around through that lens! It becomes a world full of possibilities rather than just problems. It was only later, when I wanted to be an artist, that she asked me if I'd be able to make a living doing that. Really good question!

Mom was our fierce defender, as well. If Dad got some crazy notion about how to treat us, she would get him to back down—and he seldom backed down from anything. She put a lot on the line to defend us. One time, I know she told him that if he continued treating me as he was doing, she'd divorce him. Sometimes it takes a big wrench to turn a stubborn fitting!

Life wasn't easy for my mother. From her own father's early death, to having breast cancer at thirty, to taking care of five kids (only four of whom were young), to having a doctor-induced stroke at fifty-eight that put her in a wheelchair for the remaining sixteen years of her life, she was challenged at every stage. Still, after all that, she remained bright, optimistic, and always glad to see a friend. After the stroke, she was paralyzed on one side and couldn't really speak. Most of her "friends" fell away; it seemed they couldn't deal with seeing her so changed. But when her college roommate found time over the years to come visit, every time they'd both just light up with joy.

Mom demonstrated her flexible strength very well. Even in her final years, she was always looking for ways to ease the burden on others. If someone was uncomfortable, she would give them a big smile and happy sounds, showering on them the comfort they needed. She would gesture and encourage folks to have a seat. She always made it clear somehow that she wanted to know about them and what they were doing. I'm not trying to make her sound superhuman here; she had weaknesses too. But, taken as a whole, she demonstrated to me and others how to live well, no matter what. She lived her life around what counts. I think I got the lesson.

One of the best gifts she gave me is that no matter what question I may have for her now, I know the answer—and I can hear that answer, spoken in her voice. So, for me, she hasn't really left. She built me of herself, and she lives through me, and through other people too. Whenever I meet someone who knew her, they talk of her with such gratitude. They tell me that they can see Mom in my eyes and ways of being. I can't imagine a greater compliment! Her examples keep on giving. Love is an amazingly powerful force!

 Work to stay healthy–physically, mentally, spiritually. These are your foundation.

Pancakes

I had pancakes this morning, and they were good. On the pancakes, I put the last of the maple syrup from the bottle you see here. It's a storied bottle, and it made me think back to how it came into my possession.

For years, I had a friend named Gary. He was a radio guy, and amazingly good at hosting a talk show. His ability to bring people out during an interview was stunning to hear. I recall one interview in which he brought a retired police officer to tears, just remembering what that officer had been through. It was something that surprised even that retired policeman.

It's hard to sum up Gary…maybe you could call him a perfectionist with foibles. He was a big dreamer. One of his dreams was to create an interactive community for locals in his town. He thought of a way to use the internet to bring everyone together and be able to show what they were best at and wanted to be known for. This would have helped people to get to know each other better and also bring in people from out of town to enjoy what the locals had to offer. We never got that project off the ground, as too many people couldn't easily see what benefit it would have brought. I suspect that naysayers are a common problem for big thinkers and dreamers.

In the end, cancer got Gary. He'd been quite the athlete before, but I vividly remember seeing him for the last time; shrunken, frail, and so needy. After he died, I helped his very patient ex-wife (with her wicked good sense of humor) clean out the home Gary had lived in. It took days to get down to bare floors and cupboards. One of the things we found in a cupboard was this bottle of maple syrup, which I got to bring home. Every time I enjoyed the maple syrup in the bottle, I reflected on Gary and what I learned from his life. He was so good at connecting with people, but I've always been on the shy side, so I have found genuinely connecting with others hard to do. Gary seemed to be good at being present and making the most of any situation. He was seldom lost in his thoughts and unable to do what needed doing right at that moment. I'm better now, but used to "study on" things quite a lot before taking action. I've learned there is a place for consideration and also a place for action.

As I said, cancer got Gary. He looked to be in good health, but it got him anyway. When I was younger, a diagnosis of cancer was a death sentence. Now, it's not quite so clear, but it's still not good. Treatments are horrendous and often don't work. What can be done? What can I do?

Most of my adult life, I've tried to be useful to others. For years, I did it by helping people out using my technical knowhow. I fooled them into thinking I know something about hot water and maybe a bit about energy, too! Now I've been around long enough that I've seen far too many lives cut short without need or reason, and Gary is a good example. He had a lot more to give. Also, friends now suffer with all sorts of ailments that doctors just call "getting old." Growing old really ain't for sissies in the U.S.! So my question to myself is, "How can I be of greater service?"

The health problem is obvious, and the answer is simple: Learn about life, and about what makes life strong and durable, then put it to use!

I recently completed a 100-day training in Siddha Veda. Practitioners of Siddha Veda see the human body quite differently than Western doctors do; they look at whole body systems and seek to understand and treat the root cause of disease. The treatment depends greatly on what your constitution is, so treatments must be tailored to each individual. The ancient Indian and Chinese healing approaches have similarities, like a very broad perspective on health, and can be used to good effect in conjunction with Western medicine, or where it comes up short.

What really matters in the end is what actually works. I've learned of tools that can have a profound and beneficial effect on those who are willing to try them. I love being able to help with hot water, but being able to help with people's health, happiness, and hope is orders of magnitude greater! If I'd known about this sooner, I might have been able to help Gary overcome his cancer.

I'm just starting on this journey of learning about Siddha Veda, but the potential for good is so big that I'm eager to share it with you. I encourage you to look into Siddha Veda for your own health and happiness, and that of your friends and family. The best introduction I know is a book called *Ancient Secrets of a Master Healer* by Clint Rogers. It has helped push me from my old comfort zone of only trying to help people with technical know-how into this new arena of the vast world of human health. Although I'm pretty sure I've saved lives by making water heaters less of a hazard, I'm looking forward to helping people get their health and happiness back by bringing some ancient healing ways into the present for all to see.

I'm not so young anymore, but using some of the Siddha Veda techniques has helped get me back in shape, be more alert, and have many fewer aches and pains. There's just nothing like personal experience to make some ideas real. I do wish it hadn't come at such a high price, but that was some really good maple syrup Gary left me!

Quiet Time

I never realized the power of quiet time until I went too many years without it. I didn't understand its healing properties, or how it gave me clarity, even in potentially confusing situations. When I was much younger, I needed to set aside quiet time just  so I could make sense of the world and be in it. Then I got older, took on responsibilities, and put others' needs before mine. I'm only now seeing the error of my ways!

We live in a very busy world. It's full of things to want or get upset about. It's full of misinformation and information to sift through. It's got machinations and gyrations. Now, with the internet, we all have instant access to all of it, and everything wants your attention. Overwhelm seems inevitable. Quiet time is the thing that puts control of our lives back into our own hands, and it seems to work better than any drug or supplement!

Recently, I've been getting forgetful and misplacing things. I've been nagged by always wondering what I'm missing. I'd head out and then remember something I'd planned on having with me. Maintaining focus was requiring more effort. Stuff like this makes me wonder if my mind is slipping, and that's not at all a comfortable thought. I've been taking mind support supplements, and they seemed to help, yet being on the edge of overwhelm is where I've spent too much of my time lately. Then Quiet Time knocked on the door and asked to be let back in.

Let me introduce you to Quiet Time. Quiet Time is there for all of us if we make time and space inside for it. Similar to meditation, Quiet Time means quieting your mind so that there are no more words, feelings, images, or whatever else wants to occupy your mind. Paying attention to your breathing is a good technique for inviting Quiet Time back. Visualizing a light with your eyes closed and focusing on that light is another way. I've found with breathing that at the end of each exhalation is a quiet spot. Just breathe for a bit and feel those spots. Now think of those spots as pearls on a string, all separated a bit. Keep breathing and help the spots to grow. Watch them grow bigger and bigger until they overlap and all join into one continuous stream of quiet. Or listen only to the sound of crickets. This isn't hard to do. With practice, you can be wrapped in internal quietude in just five or ten minutes.

Now the fun begins! Your mind is quiet and there is space. It's no longer cluttered with all that noise and distraction. With all that quiet space, something just falls in. That something may be as simple as a chore you wanted to get done but forgot, or it may be a "new" thought about solving a troublesome problem for a friend, or a very different perspective on someone or something. Creating quiet lets your mind share with you what's unconsciously been going on. For me, a number of surprises had been waiting for an opportunity to show themselves. But that's just half of the story.

The other half is that once my mind was allowed to release some of the caged thoughts, it became more present, clearer, and smarter! I'm putting in my quiet time twice a day and it feels like what happens when you feed a starving dog. That hound is instantly happier and gets some energy back. Quiet time is working far better and faster than any brain supplement I've ever tried. I put in anywhere from fifteen minutes to an hour, twice a day, getting to that internal quiet space. I've got better focus, far less forgetfulness, and generally feel better about myself and my brain. The worry about early onset Alzheimer's is fading.

When I was a kid, I was smart enough to know when I needed to stop and get quiet time. As a grownup, I just powered through so much that powering through became the norm. I think I'm gonna listen to my inner child more seriously from now on. He had some good and important tips for living well. Heck, maybe it's time to have fun and just play!

 Practice simply listening to others while quieting the internal noise.

My Other Father

When I was fourteen, my father's friend and partner, Stan, offered to hire me to come work at some apartments he owned. I wanted to be involved in the "real world," so it felt good to be in it and working. I was expensive, starting at $1.50 an hour. 😊 Once, I was mowing the lawn and Stan was praising me to some friends of his, telling them how I was giving the lawn such a nice, smooth haircut. It made me focus harder on getting it right. I wasn't going to give a so-so haircut after that! It didn't take long for Stan to give me a raise to $1.75. I sure felt appreciated! Pretty soon, I was being taught how to fix faucets and other plumbing, to understand and deal with electrical stuff, and do woodworking jobs. I soaked it all in. I began to feel my hands had their own language that was far more articulate than what just words could express.

Stan encouraged me along the way. After a few years, he was asking me for my ideas on problem solving. It was a single question he posed to me that really did change the course of my life. There was a noisy water heater in an apartment and the tenant was unhappy. Stan asked me if there was anything I could do. I thought about it for days. I knew it was sediment sitting on the bottom of the tank that caused the problem, but there was no effective method in existence to quickly remove that sediment. So, I got a milk crate, put a pump and filter into it, created a "wand" that would go into the tank from the top, and made a water-based vacuum cleaner to pull the sediment out and return the hot water back to the tank. It worked! The tenant was happy, but more importantly, it led me on a quest to learn all about water heaters. More than forty years later I'm still on that quest, but in the meantime, Stan benefitted from what I learned about how to make heaters perform and last a long time. Many others have, too. He asked a very good question!

Stan continued challenging me in different ways by coming up with interesting problems that needed fixing. One time, a beam supporting a two-story apartment building was rotting. How do you fix or replace something like that without moving everybody out? With the help of an engineer, I figured out a way to rebuild the beam in place. It took a twenty-ton jack and some creative platform work to spread out the load, but I was able to raise the building back up and make it sturdy without anyone having to leave. A few times, there were main line water leaks where we really didn't want to shut off the water. It is possible to clean up the pipe and get a repair clamp in place while the line is under pressure. I did get a little wet doing this, but I got it done. Then there were drain lines that nobody could unclog. Even running a snake didn't work because the plumbing had been built with a type of plumbing fitting called a cross rather than a double wye fitting between apartments. The result was that the snake would go down the drain and come up in the apartment next door. Such excitement! I figured out a way to use two expanding rubber drain openers at once to force the clog down the drain. Stan nurtured my creativity in interesting and useful ways!

Stan and my biological father were friends and business partners. Each one brought their own skills to the game, and it worked. One time Stan took me aside and said, "Your father and I have a handshake agreement. We've had it for fifty years now, and never once have either of us raised our voice to the other."

And then he chuckled, with a smile. Lawyers can draw up lengthy partnership agreements, but people will always find ways to mess things up and be unhappy. Expectations can so easily cause such arrangements to sour, but that didn't ever happen with Stan and my father. They respected each other along with understanding each other's talents. I imagine some flexibility was needed at times. To me, a handshake agreement is the gold standard for partnerships. You just need to be able to truly see and understand your partner.

Years flew by and my father passed on, leaving me as Stan's new partner. I was absolutely not going to let him down, or not be up to the job. We got to work together for a few years, and I know I carried my weight and took some of the burden off of him. It felt good to be able to give back to someone who had given me so much. Through my involvement with Stan, I learned so much more than a basic understanding of how to fix things. I got to stretch my wings in creative ways while being appreciated for it. I learned self-confidence from the challenges he handed me. I got to see how a great partnership can be, and then step into the big shoes when the time came. I got to see the power of being able to listen and then come up with appropriate actions. Like a good father, Stan taught by example, asked good questions, and helped me gain the maturity and strength needed to be a useful part of society. Stan was a grounded man who had no enemies and everybody respected. He truly earned that regard!

Stan made it to 100 years, then left peacefully. One of his biological sons told me that, "He was in good spirits right up to the end."

There are some people in this world who you know right away that you are fortunate to know them. Stan was one of those people for me. Like the North Star, Stan shone a light that made my path easier to see.

 The Golden Rule (Do unto others as you would have them do unto you) is worth remembering.

Being Helpful

I don't know how I got this way, but I like being helpful. It's been a way of life for me for a long time. I get some satisfaction from making a difference, which probably helps me as much as I help others. For example, little plant starts I helped my Mom put in the ground when I was a kid are now good-sized trees; she's gone, but the trees help keep us connected.

In my work, I solve problems for people; I make their equipment behave better, last longer, and generally cost them less grief and money. That's not bad. I've come to really enjoy troubleshooting, which could be called the art of figuring things out and creating solutions. Troubleshooting can happen in all sorts of different fields, and it's one form of being helpful.

So, imagine life for me, who likes to be useful to others, when I'm "handed" a tool that can allow me or anyone to be far more helpful... more helpful than I'd ever imagined. If you could use this tool to give people their lives back, essentially turning the clock back, or even giving them their life back when they thought their time was up, wouldn't that be an amazing tool to wield?

I've noticed that a lot of people are not well. Have you seen this? Some are really not well. I had a friend named Dave, who I knew for fifty-five years, and he looked to be in good shape. He died a few weeks ago, driving home the point that life is fragile. Wouldn't it be a powerful good if we could help each other to improve our health? I knew Dave longer than I knew my own parents. I'm motivated! Think about this. If you had a friend with a disability or long-term health problem that Western medicine could only treat symptomatically, and you had a way to actually cure that ailment, wouldn't it make both of you feel wonderful? To me, this is orders of magnitude greater than helping people with their mechanical equipment.

For example, I just finished taking taking a 100-day Siddha-Veda trainng. At the beginning of the course, we were asked to identify our own physical conditions that we would like to improve. During the training, we got to learn about and try different healing practices to explore how they work on our very own selves. I got a number of benefits; my favorite was that the stomach pains I'd had for forty years went away! Looking forward, seeing and feeling improvements in myself makes it much easier to have confidence in helping others. My personal healing story can give them hope of making things better for themselves—and hope itself is a healer.

The healing available via Siddha-Veda goes far beyond alleviating simple aches and pains. I've seen stories of disabled people walking again, people recovering from stage-four cancers, and people with chronic mystery illnesses getting back their long-lost hope. It looks like miracles, but it's simply a science that we in the West don't understand yet.

For me, learning about Siddha-Veda has brought about a powerful transformation. Now I feel I have the tools and resources to be far more useful to others. Information from the training seems to have soaked in when I didn't even know it, because now I have answers for people when they complain about physical problems. I can assure them that it's not just "getting old," but that there are things they can do to heal. I don't need to wonder why I'm meddling in someone else's affairs when I suggest some things they can do for their child's asthma. And we have access to Indian doctors trained in Siddha-Veda, so people can get information from trained professionals.

The 100-day training was quite a ride. I went from being skeptical of their "magic" to wondering why this information isn't well-known around the world. Even if this information were only carried by snails (who could swim), it would have made its way around the globe many times in the last few thousand years! I'm not at all into conspiracy theories about money or power, but when a friend with a blood disorder tells me that it will cost over $17,000 for one dose of a medication that might help, I just gotta wonder. We'll see if Siddha-Veda helps her. It certainly doesn't come with four pages of possible side effects!

This "being helpful" stuff does require some effort. It's true that "knowledge is power," but getting that knowledge takes learning where to look and knowing how to filter out the false information. But if I help only one person or animal with what I've learned, it's worth it. With luck, I'll help many more—and wow, I'll be feeling great!!

What is a Good Investment?

That title is sort of a trick question, as the answer will be different for each person and their differing needs and skill sets. The broadest definition of investment that I've found is "an act of devoting time, effort, or energy to a particular undertaking, with the expectation of a worthwhile result." I like this definition, because some people think investing can only be done with dollars. What, then, is going to college? Aside from the money part, it's a big investment of your time so that you may become more productive and beneficial

to yourself and society. Also, I like to think of money simply as a form of energy, so the definition above can work for dollars, too.

Garrett Gunderson is an investment guru who talks about finding your "investor DNA." To me, this means knowing your own strengths and weaknesses—knowing what drives you, what feels too risky, and what you want to accomplish in this life. To get more detail on this, visit 5dayweekend.com/keep-more-money/investor-dna-worksheet.

I like this approach because it's not the same old advice we've been given all our lives; essentially "scrimp and save," which people seldom do well. Clearly, financial literacy and street smarts about investing are not taught in most schools. FYI, financial literacy is the ability to understand and effectively use various financial skills, including personal financial management, budgeting, and investing. As a nation, we have a pretty dismal understanding of how money works. As an example, in 2021, the top one percent of Americans held just over thirty-two percent of all the net worth, while the lower fifty percent of Americans held just two percent. We have a lot of improvements to make!

One of Garrett Gunderson's principles is that the best investment for you is in an area you know a lot about. Using his DNA worksheet, it becomes clear that real estate is a good fit for me because I'm comfortable with it. Also, being a contractor, I can fix up a property and increase its value, both with my hands and by applying what I know about construction and energy efficiency. I can take a building that was thought to be a tear-down and turn it into affordable housing, so I can address social needs as well; I get to help people. My father was a lawyer, but he did well with real estate because he was able to fix up legally distressed properties. So, what are you good at? What do you like doing? Can you bring those talents and interests to an area that needs them, and that will reward you for applying them?

Back to the title of this piece, have you considered that investing in yourself is probably the finest investment you can make? That investment has the possibility of paying back for the rest of your life! I've had the same Skilsaw for over forty years. It probably cost $40 way back when. I've built homes with it, and a lot of other stuff. I'm pretty sure it was a good investment! Even more important is that I've been lucky with mentors. Good people have been willing to teach me some of what they know, and those lessons continue to pay me back for the time I spent learning. My mentors invested their time in me, and I'm not about to let that time be wasted.

So, what is a good investment for you? If you think about what matters to you, what you're good at, what you want to learn, and what can help you reach financial independence, it should become pretty clear where your investment energy should be put.

 Truth is something you decide on for yourself. Others' opinions don't count.

The Stories a Photo Can and Can't Tell

You've certainly heard that a picture is worth a thousand words words. Actually, there are times when words simply cannot convey the message, so no quantity of words will work.

I'm a visual thinker, as most technical people are. We "think"

in pictures, moving ones if we're lucky. Of course, physically being there is best when trying to understand the past, present, and future of something, but a picture is a nice second best. For example, the picture you see here shows my cat Rex with his arm over young Prince, who's enjoying a little warmth and adult supervision. What the photo can't tell you is that I rescued Rex from a trash pile when he was about four weeks old…bottle fed him every three hours to keep him going…had him bond with me in ways I'd never experienced before with a feline, and too few years later, had to deal with the vet not knowing how to help him when he got sick. He died at the vet's office while I held him.

Prince is another cat from the wild, and Rex was his security blanket growing up. When Rex left (and we had to evacuate due to a fire), Prince reverted to being a skittish scaredy-cat. I'm only now slowly bringing him out of that way of being to something more comfortable. The photo reminds me of the whole timeline for both cats and my place in it. I could write far more than a thousand words and not come close to conveying everything I see and feel in that photo. There is so much history behind that photograph!

It works the same for mechanical equipment and built things. A photo may show a pretty house and give you clues about the place, but you must go snooping around that old house to get the full picture. Climb around in the attic and have a look in the basement. The house has so many stories to tell about how it was built and about how it grew up and spent its time. It will show its experience in different ways. You may see the evolution of building techniques, tools, and materials. You'll definitely see the skill, or lack of it, that the hands working on the house over time possessed. You may be able to read how well off or poor the owners of the house were at times. There may be other clues, like trash left behind that are now little time capsules of events (what is that old fashioned screw cap beer can doing in the attic?). I've found old printers' plates from the local newspaper used instead of tar paper under shingles! They gave me a very good idea about what was happening when the roofing work was done on that old house, along with telling a tale of creative scrimp and save.

Plumbing has its own ways of telling you what it's been through. From solder drips and green corrosion on copper pipe (meaning the plumber could have been in a hurry or was not very careful in cleaning up their work, particularly in not completely washing off the flux) to various valves not working correctly (often meaning that hard water scale has built up inside on the working parts), plumbing loves to tell its stories to those who pay attention. Various types of corrosion also give great clues about what the piping has seen. Simply knowing where on a pipe the corrosion or damage is tells a story of too much flow (erosion corrosion, particularly after ninety-degree bends), acidic water in copper pipe (pin-holes anywhere in the line), or leaks along the bottom of horizontal iron drain lines (slow and steady flow for years, creating a waterline and eating through the iron at the air/water interface).

I like to look at plumbing (or other things) and imagine what it's experienced and been through, then think of these forces over time. That way I can "see" better what has happened and what will probably happen in future.

I frequent a site on the internet called HeatingHelp. On it are many experienced plumbing and heating folks who help solve anyone's problems, at least as they relate to the trades. ☺ Whenever someone shows up with questions about their boiler or whatever, one of the first things the pros ask for is photos. The photos tell a story and give clues about what the problem might be. Quite often, the person asking questions is made aware of important stuff they had not considered just because of what the pros see in those photos. Sometimes the photos reveal a possible life-threatening situation the questioner wasn't at all aware of!

Just like words, photos have their limits. As one thousand words can't always do what a photo can, one thousand pictures can't always tell you what a visit to the real thing will show. There is no real substitute for putting your hands on something; seeing, hearing, and smelling the environment it lives in to encourage it to tell you more stories. Still, even a visit to see and experience the real thing can't always shine a bright enough light on the mystery of what has happened there in years past. I guess we'll just have to develop a good way to travel in time!

 Be kind always, and especially to the animals, the weak, and the elderly.

Troubleshooting: Art or Science?

The man's toilet filled with hot water again, and he was upset. In fact, he was steamed! He'd been putting up with this problem off and on for years. People he'd brought in to help had been unable to figure it out. But this was probably because they saw troubleshooting only as an art. They may have imagined that if they stared long enough and hard enough at the offending toilet, a profound and clear insight into the root of the problem would result—sort of a transcendental experience.

I take a somewhat different approach when troubleshooting hot water systems. My basic premise is that we are dealing with physics, not the woo-woo. Every action, by itself, is simple and predictable (though it can get interesting when a handful of them are thrown together). So, if metaphysics doesn't solve your problem, the following practical suggestions may help.

Gathering enough information is the key. It's important not to decide what the problem is until you actually go and look; without seeing the facts in front of you, you'll waste time trying to justify your conclusions. For starters, listen to your clients. They live with the problem and are far better acquainted with its effects than you are. They can tell you the history of the system and describe how the trouble began. (Was it around the time when their six-year-old nephew played hide-and-seek in the mechanical room?) Take it all in before setting out in any one direction.

Next, try to envision the system's various movements. Use your imagination to follow its water flow and its heat transfer. Shift into fast forward and watch the corrosion processes. Can you see in your mind's eye the plug of rust developing at each copper-to-steel connection? In the same way, watch the buildup of scale and sediment. (Could that be why the disc in that swing check valve is stuck open?) Then, pretend you're water. As Dan Holohan, the hydronics wizard, says, "Wander through the pipes. Unleash the power of imagination you had as a child."

Try running the system with a pump on and then off—or a valve open and then closed. Never assume that a part works just because it should. (Have you ever opened up a suspicious valve to find the stem broken off and the gate missing? For whatever reason, the plumber before you didn't replace the valve when the stem snapped off.) Try not to get tripped up by such mental land mines. Do a thorough examination. Don't allow yourself to be hurried. If the system won't release its secrets to you when you ask what's wrong, ask what's right. Check these items off the list you create as you find they behave correctly. Part of the fun is anticipating the results of various tests you devise.

Once you have a clear grasp of a system's functions, its malfunctions and their causes will become more apparent. You will probably be juggling a great deal of information at this point, and you'll find it easier to see if you make a detailed schematic. The more accurate your schematic, the easier it will be to spot the effects of variables such as convection or air in the lines.

Relevant information can come from more than just the jobsite; don't disdain the printed word. The answer to your challenge may actually be hiding in the instructions for a piece of equipment, or it might be waiting for you in the technical section of a used bookstore. Old books can really hit the mark with their common sense answers to "new" problems. For example, a 1951 book by Watts Regulator recommends installing tempering valves with the piping arranged with a trap or upside down "U" in a way that prevents the valve always "seeing" the heat and scaling up so it no longer can function. How many tempering valves do you come across where Watts' advice was followed?

The steamy toilet problem did get fixed. The man had two water heaters, with a hot-water recirculation line tied back into one of them. Although the tanks were side-by-side, plan changes during construction caused the cold supplies to be separated. When the recirculation pump came on, it pushed water back through the cold inlet of one tank, then around and into the other, heating the entire cold line between them. So, while cold water was expected at the toilets and other fixtures, heated water arrived instead. Once the cloak of mystery had been lifted, a spring check-valve was installed in the cold supply of the tank, which had the recirculation line attached. This kept hot water from backing into the cold line and solved the problem.

My original and somewhat misleading question was "Troubleshooting: Art or Science?" While it's clear that troubleshooting can be an art, its foundation must rest firmly on method and science. Successful troubleshooting relies on a real marriage of both art and science.

Plumbers' Tools, Old and New

I like tools! They make life so much easier if you have the right ones. With a good tool, there is essentially no job you cannot deal with, in spite of difficult plumbing. Of course, there are different tools for old galvanized  steel pipe, copper pipe, or PEX piping systems. Whatever the system, good tools make my aging arms stronger and smarter.

Pictured is a pipe wrench from 1922. It was made by the Hoe Corporation in New York, and it's my first choice for a pipe wrench when I need one for threaded connections. Why? For starters, it's automatic; there's no need to turn an adjusting nut. The wrench simply slips over the pipe or fitting, and away you go. Another benefit of this wrench is that it doesn't care if what you're wrenching on is round; hex  or square can be fine, too, as the wrench adjusts automatically. It also doesn't need to grip the pipe at ninety degrees, which lets you work in difficult places or corners with ease. Compare that with the standard Stillson wrench, which is what's commonly sold these days; it just doesn't have the range of use that older wrenches offer.

For many years, I hunted for wrenches at garage sales. But now that we have the internet—and specifically the world's biggest garage sale, Ebay—it's easier to find nice old tools at fair prices.

I take a two-pronged approach when looking for tools. First, I need to know what I'm looking for.  There are some nice books on old wrenches that I've found helpful in knowing what I want to get my hands on. Here are pictures of two of my favorites. Once you've perused the books, you 'll have a better idea of what's out there that fits your needs, and you can be more precise in hunting down these tools. That's the second prong.

Unlike most modern tools, some of the old tools are made with high-carbon steel (too hard to file); it's a real pleasure to find one, clean it up, and sharpen it with a grinder (think Dremel) so that the teeth can grab the most recalcitrant pipe.

Some tools are just fun. How about this one? Any other plumber who sees it is gonna be a bit jealous! Squeeze the lever and the jaw opens. And note that the handle seems to be designed to put a length of pipe, or cheater, on to give more leverage. That was not uncommon with the older tools.

Here's one more old tool for your consideration. It's called the Eifel Plierench. Look at what it can do: It has parallel, geared jaws, which gives you a lot of force. It's easy to flatten copper pipe with these; try that with normal pliers! The jaws are adjustable and easily replaceable with other attachments just by opening up the handles wide. The other attachments I've seen are pipe jaws, a cutter-wheel for tubing, and a longer jaw for gripping bigger things. It also has  wire cutters, a screwdriver, and a pry bar built into the handles.

New tools have their place as well, but I prefer them for different reasons. For example, I recently got a FLIR One. This is an infra-red device that attaches to your smart phone and lets you see heat or the lack of it. The tool can be quite useful in diagnosing a problem, or in simply being able to "see" things a bit differently. Here's an example of three hands: the young, energetic guy who exercises a lot is in the center, the not-so-young woman is on the left, and her spouse on the right. You can see this clearly in the brighter yellow of the young man's hand versus the cooler, purple in the woman's hand. When looking at buildings, an infrared camera can show you poor electrical connections, water intrusion, air leakage, or heat loss from pipes and ducts.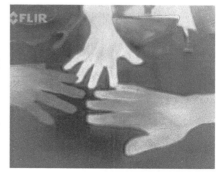

It can also make you wonder about what we "know" to be true. For fun, here's a photo of a lizard sitting on a log. They're supposed to be cold-blooded …right?

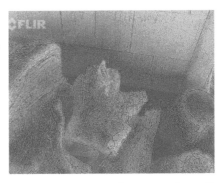

There are other wonderful modern tools: a non-contact voltage detector for "sniffing" out power in wires without needing to touch them; receptacle testers that tell you the condition of the wiring to outlets; and line locators that make tracing underground pipes and wires much easier. Another favorite tool is the gas sniffer that works better than my nose or liquid soap for detecting gas leaks (soap bubbles don't form if the leak is too fast). It works by electronically "smelling" the gas. For finding tiny leaks in gas or water lines, an ultrasonic leak detector is the thing; it hears what we can't, so it saves a lot of time.

The thing is, the larger variety of tools you carry, the better you will be able to deal with whatever the job at hand is challenging you with. The word "can't" is something I try to keep out of my vocabulary. The world of tools is big, and having the right ones makes life better. I hope I've whetted your appetite for looking into the wide world of tools, both old and new.

The Properties of All Materials

I'm one of those strange people who thinks in pictures and learns with my hands. Sometimes, it's my hands that do the thinking! As I work with my hands, I like and need to know the properties of things, whether they're man-made or from the natural world. I wouldn't build a walking bridge across a stream with rope that's too

small, stretchy, or vulnerable to degradation from sunlight, because bad things could happen. I wouldn't use greatly different metals together in a moist environment, because bad things will definitely happen! Following, you'll learn about some of my favorite sources of information about man made things and what they do. A book on corrosion engineering will tell you why it's not a good idea to mix different metals in a wet environment!

Before I was even a teenager, my grandmother introduced me to her friend Andy, who was an airplane mechanic. Andy gave me a little booklet called *Pipe Fitters Manual*, created by the plumbing fittings manufacturer Tube Turn. It has all sorts of information in it: many kinds of conversion factors, properties of metals, properties of fluids, and more. One of the fun charts is about how steel looks at various temperatures. For example, at 990 degrees F steel appears "black red." At 1,375 degrees, steel is "full cherry red;" at 1,725 degrees it's light salmon, and at 2,220 degrees the steel is white. What this chart lets me do is see the temperature of things when working with them. Black red, by the way, is when you can just begin to see a glow from the hot metal in a darkened room. It's a useful thing to remember when looking at a thermocouple in a water heater!

There's another book I like a lot, called *The Making of Tools*, by Alexander Weygers. He was an interesting guy; he even patented the concept of flying saucers! In *The Making of Tools*, he teaches how to build your own workshop, from the workbench to even making the tools you'll use on it, all in the proper sequence. He shows how to make a knife from an old leaf spring from a car, which I did. When grinding steel, he teaches you how to judge how much carbon is in the metal based on the quality of the spark. That carbon greatly affects the strength of the steel and what it can be used for. Building your own shop provides great comfort when working in it; you become the master of metal, wood, or whatever materials you prefer.

Corrosion Engineering by Fontana and Greene is another book I value for giving me a different perspective on metals. It discusses the many forms of corrosion, shows what they look like, and covers how to design things to prevent problems. Corrosion is a very expensive problem in the modern world, causing about $2.5 trillion in damage annually, so knowing how to avoid it really matters.

These books help us understand and get comfortable with metals. Reading them makes it easier to see into and understand the built environment. The fields of wood, stone, cements and plasters, glass, electricity, and many others are each rich in lore and potential depth of knowledge. Just to pick one area, cements and plasters, lime plaster has been around since Roman times, but modern man has largely forgotten about it. We use Portland cement these days. Two world wars killed off many of the tradespeople who understood how to work with lime plasters. I've seen photos of very old buildings that were not straight, but rather adjusted as the earth below them moved. They did this without breaking or being damaged at all and it's because of the flexibility of lime plaster. I think it's a good material to know about. You may be drawn to one or more of these materials. Fortunately, there are lots of resource materials available, new and old, that can help give you a quick path to the deeper understanding that makes working with your chosen materials particularly fulfilling.

I'm very interested in knowing materials well; my feeling is that if I understand materials well enough, I'll know what can be used where, regardless of what's considered normal or what something is actually designed to do. Recently, my hand-powered log-splitter broke. My options were to go get a new one (if I could find it) or to make what I had work again. I wound up fixing the splitter by remaking the spring return mechanism using a bronze floor flange that I had sitting around. Now it's back in business! I knew that the bronze flange had sufficient strength, and it made the repair pretty easy.

Put differently, just because a coat hook is called a coat hook, that doesn't mean it can't be used as a knob on a cabinet door. I did this in my kitchen, and I can tell you that it's easier to use and less expensive than most cabinet hardware. It also has the benefits of much less skin oil getting into and ruining the door's finish—and you can hang things on the hooks! Another thing I did to misuse material in my house was to take the finned copper tube that solar panels are made with and use it to move heat backwards. That is, I run warm water through the copper tubing and the heat travels out into the fins and into my house. These finned tubes were designed to collect heat from the sun and put it into water in the tubing. Well, heat doesn't care which way it travels! Knowing materials makes it easier to use them creatively AND successfully.

So, really, there are two thoughts here. One is to be comfortable in your understanding of materials in a way that goes beyond numbers. The goal is to understand materials with as many of your senses as you can…though I'd skip tasting hot metal! The second concept is to look at things made for one purpose and, by understanding their properties, be able to say, "Hmmm, I could use this pump flange to make a toilet paper holder that's better than what's at the store!"

And you know what incandescent light bulbs are good for? Darning socks! Just stick that bulb under the hole in the sock and darn away with ease. This reminds me of another great resource: a series of books written by Amy Dacyczyn called *The Tightwad Gazette*. It's subtitled *Promoting Thrift as a Viable Alternative Lifestyle*. In the *Gazette*, Amy details how to use objects in ways that are different than what they were intended for, pointing to the fact that understanding how to "misuse" materials goes a long way toward living a thrifty lifestyle.

My goal is to understand the properties of all the materials I might run across. I have a long way to go, but I can say for sure that even knowing only a little really helps when dealing with any sort of physical problem. The more you learn, the more comfortable you'll feel when dealing with the physical world because you can feel confident that you'll be able to make things work somehow, in some creative way. That alone makes learning this stuff fun!

"You've Got Me Surrounded!"

That's exactly what the guy said when I picked up the phone. "Huh?" I replied intelligently.

He explained that he had called the gas company (which has a policy of not referring contractors) to ask for a referral to a plumber who did water heater maintenance, and they'd referred him to me as the only person doing that kind of work. Then he called the water

company…same story. Finally, he called his plumber, who also told him to call me. No doubt he wondered how much I'd spent to pay everybody off! In fact, all I'd done was to work diligently to understand exactly how water heaters do and don't work, then used that know-how to help clients. I sought out the most knowledgeable hot water people in North America and shared information with them. At first they taught me, but pretty soon, I was able to give back to them lessons I had learned in the field.

Early in my career, I was a generalist. I tried to do everything that might ever need doing around a home, from carpentry to plumbing and electrical to painting and tree work. That's a great way to know only a little about a lot of topics—and spend a lot of unpaid time doing research and hunting for parts! There isn't a big enough truck to carry *all* the tools and parts you'll need if you try to do it all. It's good and useful to have a generalist's understanding of things, but understanding one topic in depth is even more valuable; it makes you the go-to person in that field. And a good reputation means you don't need to worry about whether the phone will ring. Long ago, the plumbers in my area tried to make themselves look good by dissing other plumbers. This isn't unusual, but it is unfortunate; it just makes the entire group look untrustworthy. As I was transitioning from generalist to "hot water guy," I started calling the other plumbers in town, asking what they liked to do best. When I got calls about doing plumbing other than hot water, I began to refer the work to the plumber who really liked that sort of work. A couple of interesting things happened next: I started getting hot water referrals in return, and slowly the plumbers stopped bad-mouthing each other. The latter might just be a coincidence, but it made the local plumbing world much nicer! The bar was raised. There are many paths to becoming an expert. You may remember a little book called *50 Simple Things You Can Do to Save the Earth* by John Javna (now updated and in print!). My work on hot water became one of those fifty things. I got a call out of the blue from John Javna, and we spent some time talking about hot water and what you can do to make it more efficient in a bunch of ways. John boiled it down to something that could fit into his book, which caused thousands of letters to arrive in my mailbox from all over the world. Schoolteachers particularly liked to use it as a class outline. I needed lots of stamps, because I received a lot of questions, and this was before the internet took hold. I got asked the same questions over and over, and I began to understand that people couldn't readily find good, truthful answers to their hot water questions. This became the inspiration for writing *The Water Heater Workbook*, which then changed my life some more. Being considered an expert comes with responsibility. It means you cannot stop learning; you need to stay informed so that you can give the best possible answers to those who choose to trust you.

My point in writing this is not to toot any horns, but rather to share what has worked for me and might work for you, regardless of your field. And as long as I'm sharing my thoughts on business and philosophy, there is one more thing I can say with certainty, though I still don't really understand how it works: If you take care of others, you will be taken care of. I once sat down and did the math: In a period of ten years, I had a total of just under two weeks of slow work. That's pretty good! Additionally, when trouble comes to visit, something good invariably arrives to help me deal with the trouble. Every single time. This being the case, I've learned that worry has no place to stand and bother me from. It must find me frustrating. Hmmm, I just might have worry surrounded!

When We Look for the Good

Focus on what's wrong. Surround yourself with negativity. Isn't this what we do when we pay attention only to what needs fixing? Is it really a surprise when we become worried, afraid, tired, or disempowered when we aren't balancing what's wrong with what's right?

Often, it's the simple truths that are the hardest to see. We're surrounded by "roses" of all sorts that would love to be sniffed, but we're designed to see things when they move. Otherwise, they just blend into the background. Problems are like those moving objects, too. They're like having a burr in your sock. You pay attention to the burr, rather than the rest of your foot, which is comfortable. Of course, that burr needs to come out of your sock, but it being there doesn't mean the sun isn't out, the air isn't a nice temperature, or that there aren't some smiles to be seen and animals to be petted in addition to a mostly comfortable foot! And yes, there are times when we really need to focus hard on a problem, particularly if it's a responsibility we've taken on. I don't really want the EMT taking time to smell the roses when I'm busy having a heart attack. But, almost all of the time, we have the option of balance.

Why is it that the things that are right, that could give balance, are hard to see? Are we so deep in our ruts and our ways of viewing the world that we can't see out over the edges? The media seldom tries to sell good news. They probably find it boring, so they spend time reporting on the unhappy bleeding edge. Our society has focused long and hard on what's wrong. It's what we're generally conditioned to look for. Perhaps it's deep in our genetic code that if we're ever alert to what's wrong, we're more likely to survive. But then, genetic code is also about living just long enough to have and raise children. After that perhaps we're genetically less useful to the survival of the species. Hmmm.

But since we're here, let's see what we can do to improve the quality of everybody's lives in the here and now just by noticing what's right with the world, along with what isn't. It's common to look at things and people with some dark version of rose-colored glasses. Say you expect someone to be difficult. You could avoid them or label them somehow. Alternatively, you could prepare yourself by thinking about what they are actually good at before dealing with them. You might feel a newfound respect for them and be better able to listen to and deal with them. Curmudgeonly old guys like me are the perfect test bed for putting this theory to use. How about that guy you keep at a distance because he was mean to you in grade school? Years have passed and you both have changed, but you still keep him at arm's length. Maybe it's time to see what happens if you say hi, rather than live and relive past insults. If he still hasn't grown up, or is still feeling his own pain too much, well at least you tried.

I enjoy the fun of looking for the good in everyone and everything, even myself sometimes! I like to mix a little sweet into the sour so that life just tastes better. The interesting thing that happens when you sweeten things up is that it increases your ability to deal with people or things that might otherwise seem too unpleasant to be around, or even dangerous. It deepens your well of compassion and gives you a flexible strength that is so very useful. I've watched this play out with different people and their situations over time, and it always works out well somehow. One more thing I've seen is that if you expect the best from someone, the bar is raised and they will put more effort into making good things happen. If you just "know" they will step up, they often do. It's fun to watch!

Looking for the good is a powerful way of enriching your life and the lives around you. It doesn't mean you'll be blindsided by things that go badly, just that the door remains wide open for all of that good stuff, too. Not much to lose except some bitterness!

Cat Stories

Shadow is Polite

He wants me to wake up, but doesn't want to be the one to make it happen. He understands that I think it rude to be awakened by an impatient cat. So he waits, sort of. He'd like a sign that I'm waking, because then it's OK to hurry the process. I must be careful. I play possum so he'll think I'm sleeping.

Still, he needs to test and see if I'm really asleep. He begins by head-bumping my hand, which is hanging off the side of the bed. I don't react. He tries it six or seven times…still no reaction. He even tries the cold-wet-nose approach on my hand.

Next is to try the little-sharp-claws trick. This is where he finds some bare skin, like my arm, and puts one front paw on it. Then, slowly, he extends his claws, adding a little pressure, just to see what happens. Do I jump? Do I move his little sharp claws off my skin?

If I manage to lie still through that, he's on to the fourth technique. He comes up to my face and sniffs around. It's hard to miss, which you'll know if you've ever had a critter's furry face up against yours. Then he starts licking my mustache. Try ignoring that! I do manage and, after a bit, Shadow decides that I must actually be an insensitive lump and walks down to rest against my leg, leaning into me with his back.

He's such a good kitty that, after a few minutes, I raise my hand. Right away he's there to get petted and welcome me to the land of the living! He continues to remind me that, given the opportunity, cats and other animals will demonstrate their unique personalities just as plainly as their human counterparts do.

Mama Cat Walked Out

I doubt that it was her intent, but the opportunity presented itself. It seems that my wife (who has never been the same since a stroke years ago) wasn't paying attention and opened the door—and Mama slipped out unnoticed. I was working out of town at the time. When I returned home, my wife casually mentioned that she hadn't seen Mama Cat for a few days. I searched the house thoroughly, and found no sign of Mama.

I have little hope of ever seeing her again. It's hot and dry, with no water outside, and there are predators—bobcat, mountain lion, coyote.

Mama Cat wasn't cuddly, but she was amazingly polite and tolerated me rather well. It hurt to have her yanked from my life, and probably will for some time. I still scan the hills when coming or going, just in case.

I could rationalize that Mama Cat probably had a better and longer life than she would have if I hadn't trapped and brought her home from her feral existence, but that doesn't change what is. People usually live longer than their pets/fellow travelers, so we expect to have to deal with loss at times. But this came without warning, and there was no way to prepare for it.

My main wish is that somehow Mama Cat is at peace with things, whatever that may mean. I'm not. I take it as my responsibility to give the animals a long, happy, peaceful life, and I don't know what I'd do differently to prevent this. It's one of those "real life" events that makes it hard to pay attention to my innocent and optimistic inner child, but rather easy to hear the jaded and unhappy inner curmudgeon. I hope that, some day, the spirit of Mama Cat will come back to me in some form and try again.

Memories of Merlin

I found Merlin in a litter of kittens at a home in Carmel Valley. The people who lived there were looking for good homes for the kittens. I'd come looking because I'd endured a series of deaths in my family, and I was hoping to find some magic to help. I just sat and watched the kittens as  they played on the floor. Merlin was clearly the boss. He seemed scared of nothing, not even me—so he came home for the next sixteen years. He was so clearly an intelligent one. He loved to play, and would even fetch if I did my part right.

I've come around to not naming pets until I've lived with them for a bit, and at some point their name comes to me. The name I receive is based on the many ways in which animals share their personality (catality? dogality?). Merlin was magic. He made me focus on life rather than death. He gave me reason to look forward rather than backward. He helped me learn the power of being present in the moment, as opposed to spending too much time in the future or past. After all, one can only find satisfaction in the present.

Merlin certainly had his instincts to deal with. One time I caught him with a hummingbird in his mouth. I squeezed his cheeks between the jaws, loosened his grip, and let the bird fly free. Merlin kept trying to catch hummingbirds by sitting quietly on the edge of my roof just above the hummingbird feeder. When a bird flew up and past the roof, he'd reach out and try to snag it. I fixed that by trimming the nearby tree away from the roof, giving hummers a safer place to fly.

But Merlin needed something to do, so he switched up his game and started showing an interest in the vitamin pills I took with breakfast. A rolling pill is good for chasing, and Merlin was good at making pills roll. He never ate any, he just wanted to chase them.

Merlin lived well right up to the end. I had been on a construction site, and found a bunch of newborn kittens in a trash pile. I couldn't just leave them, and ultimately brought three of them home. Merlin clearly took this as a sign that his responsibility to care for me was over and he could pass the torch on to the kittens. So he stopped eating or drinking. I took him to the vet, who gave him fluids, but Merlin clearly was having none of it. He had decided it was time to go. Merlin died at home, warm and cared for, purring occasionally. Such a magical cat needed and deserved a peaceful end. But still, I couldn't help but cry when I buried him.

The Rex

I have learned that every animal has a distinct personality and must be treated with the respect and gratitude that is their due. Rex was a perfect example.

Rex means king, and that's who Rex was. Brother of Shadow, son of Mama Cat, I brought Rex home as one of the litter I mentioned in a previous cat story. The kittens needed to be bottle-fed at first; they were that small. Rex and Shadow both fit comfortably into one of my hands. Rex bonded with me, so he had no fear; he knew that he was the chosen one.

Rex lived to have fun, to explore, and to be taken care of. He grew up afraid of nothing. And Rex was kind. When he was about five years old, two more kittens came into my life and Rex was the one these kittens cuddled up to. He'd put a paw on them as they slept, and seldom needed to correct their behavior.

Rex was always careful not to poke his claws into me. He seemed to understand other perspectives and act accordingly. If I looked at him—just looked—he'd start purring. He had a good purr motor! Lying on my chest, his motor was easy to feel. He was smart, too; I have lever handles on my doors, which he figured out early on. Every door was open to Rex, as it should be for the king.

Being in California, fires are a very real threat, and we had to evacuate when a big fire came too close. After we moved back home, Rex was still stressed and quit eating. The vet was unable to turn things around, and Rex left this place—at least physically. It's still hard to be philosophical about his going.

 Find ways to connect with animals, as they always give a lot back.

Plumbing

The Philosophy of Good Plumbing

It's helpful to follow some guiding lights when designing and building good plumbing systems. The basic concepts are simple:

1. The system should meet the needs and wants of the occupants

2. The system must be safe

3. The system should be energy- and water-efficient

4. The system should be simple and durable

The first point sounds simple, but did you know that over seventy percent of the hot water uses in most homes do not deliver hot water? Who is willing to wait for hot water when rinsing hands? Most of us aren't, but we turn on the hot tap anyway, and finish washing up before the hot water arrives. All this does is put hot water into the lines, where it just cools down to nobody's benefit.

As for safety, have you ever done the "shower dance"? That's when you're showering and someone flushes a toilet, unbalancing the system and giving you a jolt of hotter or colder water, causing you to do some quick breakdancing moves away from the shower water! In addition to being inconvenient and unpleasant, such unsteady temperatures can lead to life-threatening falls. In 2011, AARP published an article "Beware

The Most Dangerous Room In the House," which stated that each year in the U.S., there are about 188,000 injuries requiring an emergency room visit due to falls in the bathroom, many around bathing. If you have to do the shower dance, now is the time to install a pressure-balancing shower valve!

My next point about safety: Uneven temperatures can lead to falls, but they can also cause scalding. Old and very young people may not be able to sense or communicate it when they are getting burned by water that's too hot for their skin. This is another reason to install a pressure balanced shower valve. Someone flushing a toilet in another room can unbalance the shower and cause someone to get burned.

Another thing that plumbing can give us is bacteria, (or as plumbers call them, bad bugs) such as legionella, which can cause Legionnaire's disease. The balance between scalding water and harboring disease is something that the plumbing community has been struggling with for decades. Temperatures over 130 F effectively deal with most bad bugs, but that temperature can also burn people in just a few seconds. This problem can be addressed by installing anti-scald shower valves and mixing valves, but ultimately education of the general populace is probably the best defense so that people don't unknowingly put themselves in harm's way.

This leads to the next "good plumbing" topic: how to be both energy- and water-efficient. Probably the first thing to keep in mind when looking for efficient plumbing systems is to keep the volume of water between the water heater and the end use as small as possible. Why? Well, if there isn't a lot of cooled water in the hot water line, you don't need to run as much water or wait as long for hot water to arrive. Also, you haven't spent as much money to heat water that simply cooled off in the pipes. One can reduce volume by having shorter or skinnier pipes—or both! Using shorter pipes means putting all of the "wet rooms" (kitchen, bathrooms, laundry room) close together and keeping the water heater nearby, as well. That's best done in new construction or when a "gut remodel" is being done. But you can use skinnier pipes when it's time to re-pipe your house—or just because you're tired of waiting for hot water. A rule of thumb is that for every increase in size of piping materials, you roughly double the volume of water in the line. So, conversely, if you go from 1/2″ to 3/8″ pipe, you've cut the volume of water in half. That means you'll wait half as long to get hot water! It also means you will need to heat only half as much water. So you'd get a fifty percent savings by reducing your pipe diameter—and that's without even adding insulation!

But now that I've used the "I" word, let's think about what that can do for you. My friend and colleague Gary Klein wrote an article in which he goes into some detail about the benefits of installing insulation. His main point is that good insulation will slow cooling of the piping (and the water in it) so that, after the first draw of hot water, water in the lines remains at a usable temperature for much longer, essentially giving you hot water immediately on subsequent draws. This also saves water, which matters a lot in some areas. You can find Gary and a lot of good information by searching for "Gary Klein hot water".

It seems that most plumbers don't carry a pressure gauge, but they should! It's a necessary tool for achieving plumbing that is both energy- and water-efficient. If you know what the static water pressure is, you can size the piping appropriately to the use. If you install a really low-flow showerhead and you know what the water pressure is, you'll know just how small the piping or tubing to the shower valve can be. I would not be surprised to find lots of places where 1/4″ tubing would be sufficient to supply a shower with good pressure if you had a not-too-long run of tubing. Water in a smaller tube flows more quickly, scrubbing off biofilms that can harbor those bad bugs that we don't want. There are many benefits to using right-sized plumbing, including lower cost to buy and install. How does that relate to my final topic, being simple and durable?

Every piping material is good for a certain flow rate through it before any damage happens to the pipe. With copper, it's about four feet per second. If you exceed that rate, erosion corrosion begins to happen. It's like running sand through the line; the pipe gets worn down internally, becoming thinner over time. Eventually you start to get pinhole leaks. For cross-linked polyethylene (PEX), the maximum flow rate is more like ten feet per second before damage starts, because it's smooth on the inside (but this is affected by what sort of fittings you use). So, if there is adequate pressure, using small-diameter PEX tubing can give you good flow without affecting the life of the tube. PEX has a number of benefits which I talk about in detail elsewhere, but for revamping plumbing in an existing building, it's almost certainly the best choice. Also, it's much easier to run PEX than rigid pipe, as it can be snaked through walls much like wiring. Another thing about using resilient PEX is that it helps reduce the problems of water hammer (pressure surge) and freezing. It can expand slightly when necessary to take up some of the shock of caused by water hammer, or enough to allow ice to form without splitting the tube. When the hammer or freezing is done, PEX returns to its original size with no damage. That sounds pretty durable to me! PEX is still not freeze-proof, but is much more tolerant of freezing than copper. Good design can help by keeping the piping away from areas more subject to freezing. Good design will also keep the system simple, so that there are fewer moving parts to get stuck or fail.

The four categories listed above each influence the others. When thinking about good plumbing, it helps to take your time and make sure you have enough information to be able to meet all four goals. Then you can think about other important things, like cats!

The Chemistry, Physics, and Biology of Plumbing

Clean, safe water is what we expect and need to have running from our taps, but there are a number of things that can get in the way of that goal. I'm not a scientist, just a plumber who brings field experience to the discussion of safe water.

So, what are some ways in which water can become unhealthy for us? First, water (also called the universal solvent) can pick up some of whatever it touches. Water is creative and has a number of ways to do this. If it's running through copper pipe, for example, it can pick up some copper and you can ingest it. If it sits in a copper pipe for a long time, it can even deliver unhealthy amounts of copper in your water. Some copper in your diet is good. The Food and Drug Administration says you should have two milligrams daily. That said, you don't want more than 1.3 parts per million of copper in your drinking water. You can find out what's in your water by taking a sample to a local lab for analysis.

The **Plumber Protects the Health** *of the* **Nation**

Or let's say you soften your water. This basically means replacing the "hardness" of calcium and magnesium with salt. Too much softening can strip the protective layer of hardness off the copper pipe, or prevent it from forming altogether, exposing the copper. The water itself might be "hungry," which means it's so clean and free of hardness or other stuff that it's more aggressive in wanting to dissolve whatever it touches. Distilled and rain waters are good examples. So, both over-softened and naturally soft waters speed corrosion of the pipe, and you know where that loose copper is going: straight out of the tap into your drinking glass!

If you've just remodeled and installed new copper pipe—and you soften the water—wait about six months before using the softener again. This will let a thin film of scale build up on the pipes and protect them. The National Association of Corrosion Engineers suggests leaving sixty to 120 parts per million of calcium and magnesium hardness in the water after softening to prevent pipe damage.

And there are several other interesting ways to damage copper plumbing and put the residue into your water glass! Acidic or corrosive water itself can eat up copper. If you have copper pipe that was soldered before 1978 using leaded solder, that lead might make it to your tap.

Lead has long been known to damage our nerves and brains. It's thought to be a factor in the downfall of the Roman Empire! If water runs too fast or too long in the copper line—for example, a recirculation line with an oversized pump that's always on—you'll get erosion corrosion, whereby the copper is abraded away and into your drinking water. Treated nicely, copper is amazingly durable and long-lived. We just need to know how to be nice to our copper pipes. The Copper Development Association has lots of good information about how to do this.

If the brass fixtures in your home are older, the water can pick up lead from that brass. First thing in the morning is always a good time to let water run for about fifteen seconds before filling your glass, as that water has been sitting in contact with brass all night; testing has repeatedly shown that the first flush of water can have high lead levels in it.

Even galvanized pipe, which is steel pipe coated with zinc, can have some lead in it, too. Lead helps the molten zinc flow better to coat the pipe nicely. I understand that some jurisdictions no longer allow galvanized pipe to be used for water lines because of this.

Another interesting way bad stuff can get into the water is by traveling through the walls of the pipe! This can happen with PEX pipe that's buried in the ground. If the prior owner of your house used lots of weed killer or loved working on cars, the pesticide or automotive fluids could leach through the plastic pipe into the water. This is a good reason to never directly bury PEX; always run it in conduit. That can make servicing the line easier, and it keeps the sun's UV rays away from the PEX where it comes up out of the ground.

Also, plastic pipe such as PVC has plasticizers in it, which can get into the water. And PVC cement can often be smelled and tasted in the water after working on the pipes. Yummy!

Let's imagine that you have hot water in your house (it's not uncommon). The hot water comes from a water heater. If it's a glass-lined, tank-type water heater (most are), there will be a sacrificial anode rod in the tank to keep it from rusting. If that anode is made of aluminum (many are), it will be putting aluminum corrosion byproducts in your water. Being a curious person, I had water from the center of an undisturbed tank tested for aluminum—and found double the California EPA limit for aluminum! In addition, years ago, I found an interesting booklet from a doctor advising that people not use aluminum cookware. It's sobering. If you go to HeatingHelp, you'll see that booklet in their museum. I have yet to see aluminum pills in health food stores, as it's known to be a neurotoxin! So think about replacing that anode with a magnesium one, or even a power-driven one. Also, being a cautious person, I like to think about potential health hazards as "guilty until proven innocent." (See discussion of the "Precautionary Principle" below.) Magnesium pills are available because of the health benefits they bring. Yay! This is a little hint that magnesium anodes might be safer to use.

So far, I haven't said a word about bacteria, (which plumbers refer to as bugs) who really like the insides of pipes! And we are getting better at building plumbing systems that encourage the bugs to live long and prosper. This is, in part, because we oversize the lines for the actual use they get. Plumbing codes (which are primarily about making piping systems that move water) and energy codes (which are about making systems energy efficient) don't seem to talk with each other, so we size pipes according to the plumbing code—for flow rates much higher than the pipes ever see. There are circumstances in which a 1/8″ tube would meet flow requirements, yet 1/2″ lines must be installed by code. With big lines and low flow, biofilms and the other bugs that live in them have every chance to flourish. So you know, biofilm is a thin, slimy film created by bacteria that adheres to a surface. In this case, the inside of water pipes.

One reason why the plumbing codes are so out of whack with reality may be that, long ago, we had only steel pipe to play with. Plumbers knew that over time, the pipes would fill with rust, so they increased the lines by one size. This way, their clients would still get decent water flow years into the future. This was done before there were any plumbing codes, and it probably shaped how codes were written. But now we have different plumbing materials and low-flow fixtures. It actually would be easier and cost less to install smaller plumbing that is safer, works better, and conserves resources. Hmmm!

Good plumbers have known for a long time to eliminate "dead legs" in plumbing. A dead leg is a branch of a pipe that has no water flow through it. This is common in remodeled piping or is created simply by using plumbing fixtures differently. Think of that guest bathroom that's seldom used. Plumbers try to get rid of dead legs because water can stagnate in these areas and make swamp water that bugs just love growing in. Oversizing pipes creates similar growing conditions while also wasting water—which may have been heated, so it's wasting energy as well. That's 0-for-three. What a deal?

In addition, galvanized pipe is rough on the inside and it only gets worse with time. (Copper is fairly smooth, and PEX is smoother yet.) The roughness gives the biofilms a toehold, making it harder to disinfect the system. It's much better to use smaller-diameter piping or tubing so that flow is faster, scouring the walls of the pipe. Following are some tricks for increasing flow in PEX or copper piping. Avoid the use of tight ninety-degree bends or other fittings that force water to turn sharply; use bend supports with PEX or long sweep fittings for copper; and with PEX, use fittings that get inserted into expanded tubing. These measures reduce friction loss and pressure drop, so you can still get good flow with smaller pipe. Also, hot water will arrive faster when there is less volume of water in the system between the water heater and the tap. Gary Klein, who I have mentioned several times, has written extensively on these subjects.

Finally, using smooth piping and having no dead legs means that the chlorine residual (or other water treatment) gets used up more slowly, so bugs are less able to grow in the lines in the first place.

Another place in a plumbing system that often encourages bugs to grow might be surprising: It's the water filter! Water flow slows down in the filter, and there are plenty of places for the bacteria to hang out and party. If your filter has a clear housing, sunlight can help to encourage the bugs. You'll often see these filters looking green, as if algae is growing there—because it is! Filters commonly don't get changed for long periods of time. That makes the bugs even happier, because they can build entire cities, rather than just campgrounds. So, if you need to filter your water, try using an opaque filter housing and changing filter elements regularly.

With all this talk about bacteria, legionella comes to mind. It's a growing concern, as annual case numbers of Legionnaires' disease have increased about fivefold in the last twenty years. This may be due in part to better testing, and in part because of plumbing design. Legionella is primarily a concern for the old, young, or those with weak immune systems. It has long been a difficult subject of discussion for plumbers and engineers, because one good way to control legionella is to turn the water heater thermostat up to 140 degrees F, which greatly increases the scalding risk. It's a tough balancing act.

In Europe, they are far more cautious about adding chemicals to the drinking water than we are here in the U.S.. They abide by something called the "Precautionary Principle." According to Wikipedia, applying the Precautionary Principle involves analyzing the effect of the interaction of irreversibility and uncertainty on rational decision-making. Irreversibility and uncertainty; what an interesting pairing! We don't know the long-term effects of our actions, such as chemical water treatment. Yet the risk of doing irreversible damage to people's health must be taken seriously, even though it might only become evident years in the future.

For example, the incidence of Alzheimer's disease is increasing; between 2000 and 2013, the rate of death from this disease has increased by seventy-one percent. If you've ever been up close and personal with Alzheimer's, you know what a nasty disease it is. That's why I remove aluminum anodes from new and old water heaters and install magnesium instead. I don't know with certainty that the aluminum is damaging people's health or contributing to Alzheimer's, but I don't ever want to learn that I could have reduced people's chance of getting that disease and didn't act.

European countries use water treatment guidelines from the World

Health Organization, which offers a book on many aspects of water treatment. It's called *Guidelines for Drinking-Water Quality,* fourth edition. While the WHO understands the benefits of chemical water treatment, they do a lot with filtration and seem to have less trust in chemical disinfectants than we do in the U.S. We do know that there are unhappy byproducts of chemical treatment, and it appears that the WHO is trying to protect people from those nasties.

There's a lot to understand and keep track of in the quest for good water. Water from a municipal water supply used to be thought of as something we could simply trust. It was seen as our right as citizens of the U.S.A., and everybody knew it! Since water quality problems in Flint, Michigan made headlines, that perception has changed. Politics got in the way of physics—and if it happened in Flint, where else might trouble be brewing? As citizens, we also have responsibilities. Why not check up on your water? Get a Water Quality Report. Water purveyors are required to produce these yearly. Read through their report on what's in your water, and if there's anything you don't understand, research it. If you want to go a step further, have your water tested, both where it comes into your home and from a tap inside, preferably before your first use in the morning. Then you'll be able to see if the plumbing in your home is creating a problem.

If the water that's coming into your home, or just water at the tap, is found to be lacking, there are lots of things you can do to make it better. Maybe just installing a reverse-osmosis system under the kitchen sink will suffice. That way you know you'll have clean water for cooking and drinking. As water becomes scarcer, we need to find ways to conserve, but this shouldn't pose a risk to the water that we take internally. And, really, what's the problem with having different qualities of water in the home, as long as they get used appropriately? We don't need to use drinking-quality water to flush toilets!

There are good resources out there to help us understand water quality issues and how to deal with them. I'll include some of those resources for those who want to take a deeper dive.

There are lots of other water treatment options available if needed. A few places to find more information include:

- The American Water Works Association (AWWA)
- The U.S. Environmental Protection Agency (EPA); search for Federal Water Quality Standards Requirements
- Consumer Affairs; look for Water Treatment Systems

As you can see, water is pretty interesting stuff! It can do all sorts of surprising things. I've given you a lot of work to do, so should you want a fun and interesting break from your labors, here's a completely different perspective on water and what it does. Look up *Secret Messages in Water, Dr. Masaru Emoto's Mysterious Experiment*. It's interesting food for thought about how water's structure changes based on the conditions and emotions that surround it.

I've given you a lot to look into, but if it helps protect health, then it's worth it! We've covered a bit about plumbing design, and metals and minerals in the water. We've looked at pathogens and biological contaminants, and we've touched on chemicals that can find their way into the water.

Moving forward, I'd start with a water quality report to get an idea of the water coming into your home and then lab testing to know what's coming out of the taps. With that information, you'll be better able to know what sort of treatment, if any, is needed. Also, as you remodel or add fixtures, you'll be better prepared to make the piping less bacteria-friendly and more efficient. Plumbers do try to protect the health of the nation, but you don't need to be a plumber to protect your health and that of the people around you!

Plumbing That Works

What would plumbing look like if it were designed only for superior performance and durability? What if simply meeting code, and designing for the lowest cost and skill level, didn't enter into the thinking when planning a system?

Let's start by thinking about what we want the plumbing to do. Assume now that I'm talking about the hot water system because I like hot water 😊. Much of what will make the hot water system work well also applies to the cold side, so these tips are good to keep in mind for all water supply piping.

I want the plumbing to deliver clean hot water quickly, in the amounts needed, and with little or no waste of either energy or water. I also want the system to behave nicely for an extremely long time without a single problem. So, no leaks, no noise, and plenty of hot water is my end goal. Oh, and I want it to be adaptable to future changes in the building. Isn't that the plumbing you want? You should shoot for something that will perform very well, giving great service for a very long time, with little to no effort from you. Why not?

What would such a system look like? To start, we'd need to know the flow rates of the fixtures, because everything else is based on those numbers. We'd find the lowest flow rates we could, that do the job at hand. That might be a 1.5 gallons per minute (gpm) or lower flow showerhead and kitchen sink, and .5 (or better, .35) gpm lavatory sinks. We might have appliances like washing machines and dishwashers that heat their own water, so no hot line would need to be run to those places. We'd also need to know the pressure in the lines when no water is moving; called static pressure. In addition to knowing those things, we would need to figure out how long the piping runs need to be so that we can understand what the friction loss will be. Friction loss affects how much water comes out the end of a pipe and with what force, so it's important to know.

The reason we want to know all that stuff first is that it will allow the smallest system to be installed. The smaller the system, both in terms of length of pipe and pipe size, the less hot water it holds. This means you get hot water faster when you turn on the tap and waste less cooled off water in the process. It's a winning situation for as long as you use that plumbing!

There are lots of variations, but there are only two main types of systems for distributing hot water. One is called a manifold system. This is where every fixture has a small line run to it from near the water heater. The other system is called main and branch. Just like a tree, there is a main trunk line with branches from it. These branches (or twigs off the branches) serve fixtures. Bigger homes typically have main and branch systems, often with a recirculation system for quick hot water. Smaller homes can work nicely with manifold systems.

Now, finally, we can size the pipe or tubing. A good (and free) tool online for this is the System Syzer by Bell and Gossett. It is designed for copper, which prefers water to flow up to four feet per second. PEX can take ten feet per second if you have adequate pressure! One last thing to consider is water quality. Say it's acidic. You wouldn't want to use copper in that case as it won't hold up. PEX is better for aggressive waters. These days, PEX is used for about three quarters of all new installations in the U.S., so plumbers are now experienced in its use.

Plumbers seem hardwired to build straight and square. Modern materials, like PEX tubing don't need that. They work best using the most direct route and the fewest fittings, so you suffer the least pressure drop (friction losses) possible. Small diameter PEX can be run more like how electricians run wiring, taking the most direct path. Looking over new construction work, before the walls are closed up, it's often easy to find ways to install the plumbing using half as many feet of pipe. Clearly done right, the benefits can be pretty big!

Following is the key to great water service: Everything we can do to reduce the volume of water in the lines and decrease friction losses will help with better and faster hot water delivery, with the least waste. I keep this in mind when looking at or working on plumbing systems. I try to find ways to work these goals in, even for remodel work. Pressure compensating aerators and showerheads will help further by keeping flow the same even when someone else uses water in the house.

One more thing most plumbers do is to insulate as little of the plumbing as possible. We seem to operate under the misguided idea that it's not cost effective. Let's look at this from another perspective. How cost effective will it be in twenty-five or fifty years? How long will this plumbing be in place? We can be pretty sure that energy and water will never come down in price, so let's design the system to not need updating during its life. Insulate all of the hot plumbing and even the cold plumbing if it's installed in a humid climate. This way, we save BTUs and prevent condensation damage, along with improving system performance. And since we're insulating, let's use thick insulation. A good rule is to use the same thickness as pipe size. 1/2″ tube gets 1/2″ inch thick insulation, 3/4″ tube gets 3/4″ insulation, and so on, up to 2″ pipe.

Another part of the fun is when the physics say you might be able to use 1/4″ or even 1/8″ tubing to supply fixtures. With a short piping run, good pressure and a 1/2 gpm fixture, 1/8″ tubing could really work! Such small tubing, with so little water in it, means you won't need to wait long at all for hot water to arrive. Yay! It also means the system will cost less than "normal" plumbing as you're using smaller tubing, which will take less time to install; you'll be saving gallons and BTUs every day. Finally, when water moves fast in the lines, it scours the inside of the pipes, helping keep them free of biofilm and bugs of all sorts. That's healthy. There are lots of benefits to rightsizing plumbing!

The fittings pictured above are officially called Swoops. My friend, Gary Klein, figured out that fittings like this add almost no friction loss to plumbing, which lets us downsize the pipes. He decided to name the fitting "Swoop." If you're installing copper plumbing, this fitting is good. If you're working with PEX, just bend the tubing as needed with bend supports or long turns and avoid as many sharp ninety-degree fittings as possible.

Not many decades ago, we used to design houses so all the wet rooms were fairly close together. This allowed the plumbing and mechanical systems to be compact, saving money and increasing efficiency. More recently, we seem to have forgotten how to do this. Wet rooms are now spread out all over the place, as far away from the water heater as possible. Still, "central core" plumbing is a concept to keep in mind when remodeling or building from scratch, as it can dramatically increase performance of the plumbing and other systems.

Taking it one step further, if you do the central core and build a small mechanical room where the machinery of the house lives, it would be simple to build spare ports into the plumbing so more fixtures would be easy to add later on. I've found that it's possible to build chases where small plumbing can go, like oversized, hollow baseboard or crown molding. This makes adding or servicing the plumbing far easier than having to rip out sheetrock and drill through or notch studs.

This is just an overview of some of the possibilities, but you see that we can do a lot to make plumbing serve our needs better and more efficiently if we can just drop some of the commonly accepted habits and limitations. Does that work for you?

Is it Ever "Just Plumbing"?

You may not be a user of tools. You may never have had the experience of spending time under houses trying to fix things. It came to me that sharing the perspective of being the one who does the work in difficult places might be interesting. I remember long ago when management at a local restaurant made the wait staff and kitchen staff trade places for a day. After that, they all had a lot more respect for each other! See if the following story has anything at all in common with that "trading places" restaurant story.

I just got out from crawling around under a seventy-year-old house where the space is tight and obstructed with plumbing, ducting, low-hanging beams, piers, and of course broken concrete bits to crawl or rest on. This reminded me, in part, of why I decided to focus on hot water; water heaters usually live in nicer places! Anyway, part of what I was doing under the house was replacing some of the old steel drain and water lines with ABS drain and PEX water service.

Some would say this is "just plumbing," but I feel it deserves a bit more respect. Let's think about what goes into installing new plumbing or making repairs in difficult-to-access places—or in any places. The technician needs to know what work is to be accomplished, how to make sure the plumbing systems wind up being efficient, what parts will be needed, what the codes and physics are around doing the work, what order the work is best done in, and importantly, how to improvise successfully. Safety and durability matter, too. Unless you keep all of that on top of your mind, your work probably won't be very efficient. So, you can see that doing "just plumbing" might actually involve a little multitasking!

I prefer to begin work by simply staring at the job to be done and pondering the variables and possible approaches until a clear picture comes to mind, showing me the cleanest and simplest way of making things happen. It's helpful to know what the "fixed points" are. These are the bits that must be a certain way, or use a particular material, or be in a certain place. Knowing these gives me places to build from and to. I've learned over time that if I just start plumbing without that clear picture in mind, I will wind up unhappy with the result; there will inevitably be something I didn't take into consideration. I've learned that if I don't have that clear picture, I shouldn't even pick up the tools!

Sometimes it's not that simple. Other people around the job may wonder how you're earning your keep when you're just sitting there. But don't let them distract or hurry you. Show them a copy of this essay! Get that clear picture in your head to work from; you'll really be working smarter and faster this way.

Of course, it's hard to just sit and stare in a tight crawl space, so in that case I must try to imagine the job without that visual help. Toting a big pile of fittings and tools around under a house isn't practical or much fun, as you can imagine, so I aim to have only what I'll need. One of the most frustrating things for a tradesperson is to have to make multiple shopping runs in a day for one job. Actually knowing what you'll need for this sort of job just may be an art form.

This is where improvisation can be a good thing. Imagine you're under that house with limited fittings. You run pipe and find that you don't have the right fitting to complete the job. Ugh! In this case, I was bringing a drain line down but found I had only one correctly-sized forty-five-degree bend—and I needed two. What I did was cut the main line and install a coupling so that I could rotate the pipe forty-five degrees. This allowed me to hook things up using just the one forty-five. Eliminating one bend made the flow path a little easier, too! That might have been a combination of good luck and lots of field experience, but I'll take it.

Plumbing frustrates and scares many people. I believe that if we slow down and recognize the challenges of doing good plumbing, we'll give it the respect and consideration it deserves. When we do this, the plumbing task at hand will become easier and much more manageable. Sometimes respect is shown by doing good prep work. For example, if you're not too confident in your soldering abilities, practice first; it'll make the challenging job of soldering under a home much less threatening. Breaking jobs down into manageable pieces and finding ways to stay in control of the job will make life nicer, too. Just imagine cutting into a pipe to learn the water wasn't turned off. That's when the plumbing is controlling you! I have a plumber friend who was the last one working on a jobsite. He had the valve at the water meter turned off, but when he cut the line, there was pressure behind it! He spent that night on his back with his boot against the end of the cut pipe. The next morning, he learned that this house had two water meters. The plumbing won that round!

Also, before you even begin any job, finding a mentor—someone willing to share tips and tricks—won't hurt either. There are plenty of older, experienced plumbers out there who love sharing their hard-won know how. Cultivate a working relationship or friendship with one of them and you'll be glad you did.

I think you know by now that it seldom is "just plumbing." There is so much more to it! Good plumbers are trying not simply to make a dollar, but to do their job well, so it serves the owner and is something to be proud of, even though it will seldom be seen. Unfortunately, plumbers have been the subject of "butt crack" jokes and disrespect for far too long. It's time to shed that image and give them some well-earned respect. Next time you call that plumber whom you showed some respect to, I bet they'll find a way to help you as quickly as possible.

 When hunting for truth, we can search or research. Research is a lot more effort, but it works better.

Pros and Cons of Different Piping Materials

Most people don't really want to think about plumbing materials. We just want plumbing to work flawlessly, forever! That's nice, but reality does intervene sometimes and we then need to understand the practical considerations so we can get closer to our goals of flawless and forever.

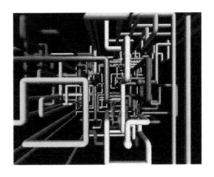

So, here we go! Each piping material has different strengths and weaknesses. Sometimes the place where piping is to be installed, or job site considerations affect which material or materials are best to use. Here I'll go over some of the considerations that help to create a long lived, efficient, and trouble-free system. I'll take it one material at a time except where there may be interactions.

To start, we're looking only at water distribution piping here. Drainage, fuels, or compressed air all have different considerations.

Let's start with Galvanized Steel pipe.

Pros:

- It's strong! It's the strongest of conventional piping materials. It even resists nails, which the other common piping materials don't.

- It is considered to be a fifty-year material, but in good water conditions can last far longer.

- As it is metal, it withstands sunlight, heat, and solvents.

- It can be assembled wet.

Cons:

- Steel rusts. When the zinc coating is used up, the steel will rust. This often builds up inside of the pipe, restricting flow and adding rust to the water.

- The galvanizing process may involve the use of lead. Lead is not good for us.

- Steel pipe is the most difficult modern material to install. Its strength and lack of flexibility make it harder to fit into place, particularly in remodel work.

- Threading also requires special tools.

- Where it's joined with brass, like at a valve, the brass will force the steel to rust away much faster.

Copper Pipe

Pros:

- Copper is far lighter than galvanized steel pipe and is easier to connect, using either soldering or press fittings.

- Soldering does require some experience to do right, but it's easily learned.
- Copper is unaffected by sunlight, moderate heat, and solvents, just like steel.
- Copper seldom builds up enough scale inside to restrict flow.

Cons:

- Unless you use soft copper, the pipe is rigid, with more flexibility than steel, but still not very flexible.
- Copper does not like acidic/aggressive water or soil. Bad water can chew through it in short order.
- It is subject to erosion corrosion, caused by water traveling too fast and thinning down the pipe.
- Nails go right through copper pipe.
- If water in the pipe freezes, it will likely burst the copper.
- It requires a torch (needs some skill) or press tool (not cheap).
- Copper has become expensive.

PVC/CPVC Pipe

Pros:

- PVC/CPVC is lightweight and simple to glue together.
- It is somewhat flexible, and easier to snake around obstructions than the metal pipe materials.
- It essentially does not scale up inside.
- It's fairly inexpensive.
- It needs no special tools.

Cons:

- PVC/CPVC does not like long exposure to sunlight, as it becomes brittle.

- Freezing can ruin entire runs of this piping, as it tends to split lengthwise.

- As it is softer than metals, it needs more, closer spaced supports.

- There is concern that it leaches plasticizers into the water, which is unhealthy.

- It cannot take the heat that metal piping can and will deform if it gets too hot, though CPVC takes heat much better than PVC does.

- Not rodent proof.

PEX Tubing

Pros:

- PEX usually comes in coils, so is flexible and requires fewer fittings to get around.

- It's the easiest material to use for retrofit construction as it flexes so well.

- It is the smoothest piping material, so can handle higher flow rates (up to ten feet per second) without damage... though the plastic fittings hold up better to this than the brass fittings.

- It can be assembled even with some water in it.

- It is freeze resistant...not freeze proof! It can expand with ice inside, but returns to its normal shape when the ice melts.

- It's a good material if you have high water pressure as it will help absorb the shock of water hammer.

Cons:

- PEX does NOT like sunlight. It must not be exposed for any significant time during storage or be installed so it sees the sun.

- Chemicals can leach directly through the material.

- PEX is slightly smaller inside than copper, so depending on flow rate, may have more pressure drop along the length of the pipe.

- It happens very rarely, but rodents can chew through PEX. It needs to be protected when run through rodent living rooms.

- PEX insert fittings substantially reduce the inside diameter of the tube, so increase friction loss. Best to use a PEX system (like Uponor) that expands the tube to go over fittings.

- PEX requires the use of special tools.

As you can see, there are things to keep in mind when deciding on a piping material. So much depends on the situation the pipe will live in and how difficult it will be to install the pipe.

As a rule, it's always easier to install smaller diameter piping. So, consider low flow fixtures when you remodel. This way you might be able to run really small stuff like 3/8″ PEX or soft copper (or smaller if allowed!). This becomes very much like running wiring because it's so small and flexible. Also, it can be put in places that larger pipe wouldn't fit, like flat raceway or hollowed baseboard.

This was just a quick overview, but hopefully it will help you to think less about and spend less time with plumbing. For fun, here's a quote from Thomas Drummond, 1797-1840: "Property has its duties as well as its rights."

What's a Cistern Doing in the Loo?

British plumbing is just as different from American plumbing as their spoken words are from ours. In a pub, in a motor car, and in the loo, language and cultural differences abound as I discovered on a trip to

England and Wales. "Chips," as in "fish and chips," aren't potato chips, but French fries. If it's chips you wanted, well, you should have asked for "crisps." If you're asked to choose between a "brown bap" and a "white bap," you're selecting the bun for your sandwich. "Boots" and "bonnets" aren't clothing, but car parts (the trunk and

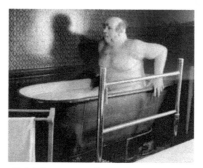

British mannequin sitting in old-style tub that was heater by a gas burner underneath.

the hood). And the cistern in the loo isn't for collecting rainwater. People travel for all sorts of reasons. For me, after working with American plumbing for years, learning about British plumbing was a natural extension of my interests. Since water heating is very interesting, that's all I was planning to study overseas. But other things grabbed my attention. I found toilets flush differently, strange drain lines poke out of buildings from unexpected places, and odd storage tanks live up in attics.

Toilets were the most accessible piece of plumbing, and they were impressive because they work so well. Their two-gallon flush has been standard since WWII (we had five-to-eight-gallon flushers then). The ball valve (fill valve) is mounted on the side of the cistern (tank). Normally, there is an overflow on the opposite side which exits via an independent pipe. This pipe may tie into the drain line through an air gap, or it may go directly to an outside wall and spill out onto whoever is there. Surprise!

The flushing mechanism is the best part. An upside down "U" acts as a siphon. Pulling the lever forces a slug of water up the U, which starts the siphon. When the water level in the cistern descends to the base of the U, the siphon is broken and flushing stops. The nice thing about this is the unit cannot leak to the drain; the big water waste we experience here with leaky flappers just doesn't exist there. I found it interesting to find in an old Crane Catalog from 1893, that a similar siphon mechanism used to be available in the U S.

But what the British gain from their water-saving toilet technology is taken away by a lack of water meters nationwide. The British countryside is lush and green, and frequent rain is a fact. But the expanding population is putting a strain on water supplies and forcing more people to seriously consider water conservation.

Unfortunately, water meters seem to be a new concept for residential use, and few places have them. Water is paid by a flat fee based on the number and types of fixtures, rather than amount of water used. I found that leaky plumbing is rampant since there's little motivation for repair. As a result, water meters could be as effective a conservation device in Britain as they are here.

In addition to plumbing, I was also tracking down good used bookstores. Old books can have a wealth of marvelous information not available in current books. Imagine my delight in discovering a whole town devoted to used books! Hay-On-Wye, on the eastern Welsh border, provided a huge number of books full of great plumbing info in the town's thirty-plus used book shops.

As I skimmed the purchases, I learned that lead water supply piping is quite common in Britain. But no one seems worried. There's no commotion about the dangers of lead. The how-to books describe how to tie into it, not how to remove it. Looking around, I judged the people there to be no balder or crazier than we are here (except perhaps when driving). It would be interesting to see a water quality study and compare actual lead levels in water here and there.

Water main distribution is also quite different. Houses have only a 1/2" supply line. That can't directly supply enough water for multiple uses and is bound to be a problem. To get around this, a large, open, unpressurized cistern (storage tank) is installed in the attic. The reason for the cold-water cistern is to provide storage for the house in the event of a water main failure or widespread high-water demand within a town or city. This cistern acts like a giant toilet tank. It has the same ball valve and overflow, and it can fill at its leisure.

As long as there is water in the attic cistern, delivery is much the same as it is here. That's a boon to the water supplier, who can use a system that would otherwise be very much undersized and incapable of delivering water "on demand" as U.S. systems do. Cisterns generally hold fifty imperial gallons (sixty U.S. gallons). That was originally about one day's usage, so water delivery would seldom be interrupted.

Having an open tank in the attic does raise concerns over airborne germs and other undesirables getting into the water. The British solution is to run a pipe from the main line (before it reaches the cistern) to the cold side of the kitchen sink. This is the only truly potable water. Everything else is suspect. An attitude adjustment would surely be needed to get such a system accepted here, for sure!

A result of having water supplied from an attic cistern is reduced pressure, so British showers are designed to operate on as little as one psi. If you don't find that sufficiently stimulating, you can add a shower pump, which boosts pressure at the shower head.

Another shower alternative is the 240 volt "geyser" (pronounced "geezer"). This instantaneous heater shares the already cozy shower stall with you. Usually, one knob selects the desired level of heating (none, low, or high), and another knob adjusts flow rate—which also affects temperature. As a result, once I got the water sufficiently warm, the flow was but a trickle. (Perhaps this water conservation technique explains the lack of water meters.) One of my lodgings did have direct supply (without cistern) and a tank-type electric water heater. The shower was strong and hot, like most American showers. I was surprised and amused by multiple warning signs in the bathroom urging caution with what they viewed as an overly powerful shower.

I also learned that British methods of heating water are different from ours. Copper cylinders (water tanks) are the norm there. I didn't find any glass-lined steel tanks. These copper cylinders hold about twenty-five imperial gallons (thirty U.S. gallons). They're covered with a rough foam insulation and may be heated with one or two electric immersion elements. (One of the "antique" plumbing books gave this interesting description of how to add an element to a copper cylinder: Poke hole in cylinder with a knife, trim hole round, insert threaded brass bushing, tin, and wipe molten lead around joint and screw element into bushing—it's that easy!) Cylinders can also be heated by a remote source, such as a boiler or even an oil burning kitchen stove.

In hard water areas, to reduce furring-up (liming), a tank-within-a-tank system is used for heat exchange. More often than not, heat exchangers, called calorifiers, are also used.

It's not unusual for the job of heating water to be spread out amongst multiple appliances. Geysers may be used at taps, baths, and showers. Washing machines and dishwashers may be supplied with built-in heaters. The need for a central heater and distribution piping disappears with all these separate units. Imagine the energy savings!

Incidentally, scorched, burnt, or blown air heating (AKA "forced air") was not something I experienced in Britain. Hydronic heating is common, and it's often connected with the domestic hot water supply. If such is the case at the inn where you are staying, and if the owner is pinching his pence, the boiler may be fired up only briefly in the morning and evening to take the chill out of the rooms. Take your shower then, or you'll be stuck with "lukecool" water later. How do I know this?

When the room radiators are hot, they're very hot. You'll see signs warning you against using them to dry towels or clothes, which could burn. The same goes for your body (and don't expect the same sympathy for poor judgment that U.S. courts have shown).

The British have learned to live happily with plumbing that has slowly evolved over a very long time. While some elements of British plumbing may seem substandard or even dangerous to us, the Brits are just as likely to look askance at American plumbing. They may very well view it (as they do our roads) as being overdone, excessive, and extravagant. In the end, I imagine that if plumbing techniques and ideas from both sides of the Atlantic were freely exchanged and seriously examined, good things would come of it for all.

I wrote this years ago and am still waiting for that wonderful toilet technology (and other ideas) to make it across the Atlantic. Plumbing changes very slowly!

Mick the Dog

A long time ago in a place very near to
here, there was Mick. He came into
my life as a small, very young puppy.
Mick was a Puli, a Hungarian sheep
dog. When fully grown, they get to be
a bit over thirty pounds with long dark
hair. That's not big for a dog, but what
Mick lacked in size, he more than made
up for with attitude. Rumor has it that
when herding sheep, the Puli jumps
from sheep back to sheep to keep the
herd in line. Agile with attitude!

As a small pup, he couldn't go far and would let his tongue hang
out, so I'd carry him. When he got a bit bigger, he was like a tractor,
tugging me around with the leash. Uphill, downhill, whatever—he just
wanted to get there sooner. He particularly enjoyed the water. Going
to the beach was his idea of a very good time! He really had an affinity
for kelp. It called to him and wanted to be tugged around. On one of
our beach trips, there was a piece of kelp in the surf line. As Mick ran
out and grabbed it, trying to get it to move, a breaker rolled in and
submerged Mick and his kelp. The water fell away and there was Mick,
still tugging on that stubborn kelp! He had a **big** attitude.

He was persistent and could even find water in a drought, but had
to work for it. He had a securely fenced back yard which I had needed
to drive steel rods into the ground under the fence because Mick would
just dig out and escape before I did so. He trained me how to make
a secure fence. So, he decided to break out screens under the house …
on both sides. This way he could escape to try and chase deer and find
water in a drought. He came back once dripping green slime and was
sooo happy! I washed him off and replaced the broken screens.

When we went driving around in my truck, Mick was keeping an eye out for cows. I'd see some in a field and would say, "Mick, cows!" and he'd let out this high-pitched squeal. He **really** wanted to meet the cows! So, one time, he got to do that. There was a cow on the other side of a rail fence. Mick went running fast toward the cow, but when he was under it, he began to realize that cows are rather big. Mick put it in reverse and came back to me pretty speedily. The cow chewed her cud and her unperturbed eyes smiled.

Mick was my helper in various ways. He'd sit in a basket and enjoy the wind in his face riding around on my motorcycle. He was good at being in the moment. He'd come up the ladder and helped me with jobs on various roofs. He could always find the most comfortable place no matter the situation. But his wild side was never far away. One night there was a small assembly of racoons on the deck behind the house, so Mick pushed the door open and charged off into the dark, chasing them. I heard a yelp and ran out making as much noise as I could, as racoons can easily kill a dog. I scooped him up and found only a slightly bloody paw. He made sure I had quick reactions.

In a very real way, Mick was my son. I raised him, learning much about parenting, patience, and kindness as he was learning about what his human expected of him and the concept of good behavior. We both learned a lot. It seems he was okay with that. When I'd come home after being away from him all day, he'd always greet me at the door, and everything from the neck down was wagging furiously.

Mick lived a long and not boring life! So many memories swirl around that dog. Even after many years, he just keeps on giving.

Philosophy

Hallelujah

One recent morning, I was in the kitchen listening to "Hallelujah," written by Leonard Cohen and performed by Rufus Wainright. There are many versions of "Hallelujah" out there, but this one is particularly moving.

I paid little attention to the other words in the song and the web they wove. Rather, I was filled with just the one radiant word, hallelujah, and the rhythm it swam in. I turned and looked out the window to see blue skies, small birds sitting in a tree, and more birds flying all about. It had rained the night before, and everything shone and glistened in the sunlight. Even the bird's beaks sparkled. Suddenly, it struck me hard and with clarity: We don't need to go looking for religion or spirituality; we're immersed in it. We're part of it! All we need is to be aware, and it flows in and through us. We simply need to say yes to it.

I thought about the stories of people who almost died, touching the fingertips of death. They experienced that light and love as they saw and felt beyond our 3D world, and I felt that same love shining in through the kitchen window.

I couldn't hold my happy tears back…or maybe I'm just crazy. Whatever, it is SUCH an amazing world we are part of. We just need to notice it—particularly when we're busy, troubled, or have no time, because those are the times when we'll get the most help from that beautiful world all around us. Finding enough quiet or internal stillness to see it seems to be the trick. It's remarkable what falls in when we quiet the noise inside and make space for good things to happen. Simply remarkable!

 Love is even stronger than "shaking in your boots" fear.

Abundance

I just listened to a talk on abundance. It discussed the mindset around abundance and money. The message was something like, "Put your mind and emotions in the right space, and money will come to you."

It's not too, too hard to visualize this happening. The message seems to be that if you "know" that money won't come to you, it simply must stay away. Focusing on the negative brings negative results. Hmmm.

This made me think of other kinds of abundance. There are many kinds of abundance, and sometimes they arrive from unexpected places and at unexpected times. Just like money, they can come to you if you leave open the possibility. So here they are, starting with some really basic ones:

- Having plenty of air when you're under water
- Having plenty of water in the desert
- Feeling peaceful in an agitated crowd
- Having internal quiet in a noisy city
- Being recognized in a bunch of strangers
- Knowing you have love in a time of fear

- Feeling understanding in a time of confusion
- Looking into a large animal's eyes and seeing tranquility, not feeling fear
- Being confident during a time of uncertainty
- Knowing the points of the compass no matter where you're facing
- Knowing you have friends even when with those you don't know
- Feeling that your loved ones never really left, even after they passed on
- Feeling accepted rather than judged
- Not feeling lost, even when you don't know where you are
- Receiving unexpected help from a total stranger

I've no doubt that you can come up with more on your own, so here are some lines, should you feel moved to write them down. Have abundant fun!

_____

_____

_____

_____

_____

_____

A Very Human Act

We had just taken off on flight 3880 from LaGuardia to Dallas, and the passenger was trying not to freak out. It looked like bad post-traumatic stress syndrome. Certainly, he was stressed. The flight attendant, Peggy, noticed him hyperventilating. She got down on a knee, put a moistened towel around his neck, and mopped his throat and chest with another towel. She pulled out her phone and some earbuds, and gave him what I imagined to be music to help calm and distract him. She talked him down from his anxiety quietly and with focus. He slowly regained some composure, thanks to her creativity and obvious care. After a bit, he was napping. What an amazing act of kindness to witness. Peggy deserves a medal. Please see what you can do for her, because she is **such** a keeper! She more than made my day.

The above is what I wrote to the airline that employs Peggy. It may have been her job, and she may even have received training in just how to do this, but I never want to ignore true, good humanity in action. It needs to be encouraged and rewarded, if just by noticing. I still carry the images in my mind of Peggy making good of a bad situation, so she also gave me a gift, which I get to share with you now.

Touchstones

I use the word "touchstones" as shorthand for things we do in relating to and communicating with others. There are useful and useless ways of doing this. Useful ones include asking yourself, before you speak, if what you want to say will help. It may feel good at times to say things

that won't help. "Told you so!" is
a common one, but what good
does it really do? You know the
answer.

Another useful touchstone
is simply (or not so simply) to
be quiet and put effort into
listening—in other words, filter

out the internal noise. Listening is an art form, and others really enjoy
being heard. Sometimes we feel that we know what the other person
is about to say, so why not help them get to the point? But if you
listen, they may surprise you. Even if they don't, just listening helps
the person who's talking feel good. They may simply feel respected,
and that's never a bad thing.

Quieting your own mind when dealing with others will help you do
a better job. Our minds love to take us on side trips; they project into
the future and imagine things that never happen. It all becomes noise
that makes it hard to hear others.

A little personal story: I've stuttered most of my life. It began
at around six, when I was told that my Mom was at serious risk
of dying from cancer. She was the center of my world, and I was
shaken. Fortunately, that cancer didn't take her. But for a while after
that, I could only communicate by writing notes. There was so much
anxiety in me that words were unwilling to come out. They'd just
stick in my throat. Years later, I figured out that if I could relax, the
stuttering would diminish or go away completely. I learned a form
of self-hypnosis that lets me get to a calm place in a second or less
so that I can control the stuttering. For me, it demonstrates one real
power of quieting the mind.

Another touchstone is patience. Grandparents are often known for
it. Seems that the more experience we have with living, and the more
aware we are of our own mortality, the better we are at being patient.
Imagine how calm this world would be if the average age of a human

were two hundred years! I'll bet redwood trees are very patient.

So far, I've been talking about things we want in life. Now I'd like to look on the other side of the fence and think about "touchstones" that we really don't want!

I'll start with expectations. This is a big one. If things don't happen, or if someone doesn't behave as we expect, then life is bad, or they are evil, or _____. You fill in the blank. Things may have gone just fine, but because they weren't as expected, we feel robbed. It's not so easy to let go of expectations, but it might be worth putting some effort into it. Maybe we fool ourselves into believing we're in control, but that's usually an illusion. Look at it this way: If you have no expectations of someone, they're not likely to do much that will bring you down. I have very little expectation of an octopus in a tank, even though I know they're a smart species. So, whether he surprises me and starts doing sign language in an attempt at interspecies communication—or just glides around in his tank—I'll be happy.

Finally, I'll throw judgment into the room. It's the elephant. Judgment is my idea of a useless rock. Western society has used judgment of appearance and other metrics to make life much harder than it needs to be for women, people of color, people too young or old, heavy people, and people who look poor. I see it as an "us versus them" approach that never helps. It only keeps civilization from becoming civil. This touchstone is powered by fear.

It's long past time to vote out fear. When we're able to recycle fear into compassion, quietness, lack of judgment and expectation, great ability to listen and love, that octopus will do a happy dance for all to see! I promise.

 Find quiet time daily. It will help remove "scattered and overwhelmed" feelings from life.

Responding vs. Reacting

This picture is a screenshot of what I get when I do an online search for "responding vs. reacting." It seems to be a hot button, so might be worth looking at a bit more. 😜

What's the difference between these two "Rs?" Hmmm. Responding to a situation or a person happens after you take in the information and stir it around in your brain and maybe your heart. Then you put forth a response that you hope is helpful.

Reacting is a very different thing. It's based on what's going on inside the listener, rather than what's going on with the teller or the message. Imagine that you tell a friend a story, but your friend seems unable to take it in, and maybe even has a dismissive response. You wind up feeling disrespected; maybe you think there's something wrong with you or that your story isn't interesting. Life isn't so good right then.

Now, imagine the same thing happens but you also learn that your friend has just discovered she has cancer, her elderly father recently fell and broke bones, her significant other spends nearly all his time playing computer games, and her dog just died. You're more likely to be able to respond to her with compassion rather than react with feeling dissed.

Everyone experiences pain some or most of the time, and just about everyone has discomfort even more often. We just can't tell how someone is feeling very accurately just by looking at them. So it's nearly impossible to know when you're truly being dissed, or simply not well heard because the other person is in some sort of pain.

People who listen well are rare and valued. What makes them able to do it? Maybe they simply set themselves aside, become egoless for a bit, and just absorb what they're being shown and told. They can then respond in a clear and focused way. I suppose it's possible that they have evicted all pain and discomfort from their lives, but it's more likely that they've found ways to redirect that energy. Samuel Clemens, aka Mark Twain, was a wonderful and amazing humorist, but that humor was counterpoint to much darkness in his life. Have a look at the lives of some of our best comedians, like Robin Williams. Do you see a trend? Maybe experiencing the bad drives us even harder to look for the good, so that we can feel some kind of balance.

It's a practice of mine to notice what's right. Looking out the window right now, sun glints off the leaves of an apricot tree, turning the leaves a bright, lime-green color. The light breeze keeps all the leaves twinkling. I wish I could paint magnificently, but I'm glad just to be able to keep such images in my head. I didn't always see the light, so to speak, but I practiced. I started by making a goal of noticing ten good things every waking hour. I hoped that this would become a habit if I did it for a while. Seems to have worked! And it didn't take very long. Now it's hard to go ten minutes without seeing ten good things.

This habit of noticing the good things has a big benefit: I'm less at the whim of discomfort or pain. That allows me to be a better listener, so I can genuinely respond rather than react. I can give people what they need. This is just how my path has taken me to being able to respond. Certainly, the path has different twists and turns for every different one of us. But for all of us, it's a path full of possibility!

Talents and Skills

Where do talents come from? We know skills are learned, but it helps to have a natural aptitude for them, too. Where does that talent come from? Well, it could be from having a high IQ, but that seems unlikely

because having more "computing power" doesn't guarantee accuracy. Maybe focusing on learning what you like is a big part of developing aptitude. When you like something, you pay closer attention to it. Then you see more about it, and you want to learn everything about it!

I'm fascinated by much of the human-made world, so am curious about how things work—how they were built, how they could be made better, and so on. Learning about these things isn't a chore to me. It's fun! From a practical perspective, I can be more useful to others when I know more about how things work. Sort of makes me think we shouldn't be pushed into learning how to make a living as much as learning about what we love, and then figuring out how to make a living with that knowledge. The discomfort of just putting in our hours and years would fade away as we began to enjoy our work.

I wish I could say where talents come from. In athletics, it's easy to see what makes a great runner, swimmer, or gymnast, but what makes someone really good in the trades, or amazing with numbers? I have a brother who, before ever going to grade school, was reading maps and had in his mind the best routes to all of his favorite places. The map inside his head now covers much of the U.S.! I don't know how he does that, but I'm pretty sure his amazing ability comes from his strong interest.

I suspect that if you learn what you like, you get better at it and more comfortable with it. That makes it even easier and more fulfilling to pursue it even more. It becomes an upward and accelerating spiral. That particular path of learning, which might be hard work for others, is fun for you!

I do think it's a good idea to know a little bit about a lot of things, but to specialize in one area—an area that really speaks to you—and then find a way to be useful to others in your chosen field and get paid for it…that's the sweet spot.

There is no hard rule saying you can't change fields if you get pulled in a different direction or find a new endeavor if it sparks joy in you. It's your life and your choice! I've come to understand that no one type of work is superior to any other type. A brain surgeon is no better than a house painter. Each type of work can be approached and executed as an art form or done sloppily. It's the person doing the work, and their love of the job and being useful, that makes the difference.

 Say only what needs to be said, and first ask yourself if it will help.

Phases We Go Through

We all go through phases. Some of them pass quickly, some last for years, and some never seem to end.

Recently, I was driving down Highway 1 near Big Sur, and saw in front of me an old concrete bridge. It fit well into the land; it was nicely framed by the hills, and there was a light blue sky above. No doubt, one could find a scene like this in many places around the world, but it took me away from my busy mind and reminded me why I've always liked the central coast of California—the place where I grew up. Despite the population having grown a **lot** in the last sixty years, the land and the ocean remain beautiful. They have many moods, and I'm happy they share these moods with me. I hope this joy is a phase I'll never outgrow!

When I was growing up, it really bothered my father that I went through phases much faster than he could grasp. I'd study something, learn a lot about it—and then, when I felt I understood the subject and it became harder to find new-to-me information, I'd find a new subject to pursue. He couldn't keep up with my interests.

As a child, I really liked figuring out how plants worked. I played with sprouting, rooting, grafting, and growing from seed. (Little plants I helped my Mom put in the ground are now good-sized trees.) But I quickly learned all I wanted to know about plants, and I moved on to studying all things mechanical. By the time I was in junior high, the teachers were asking me to fix stuff the maintenance guy couldn't get around to. I liked figuring things out then, and I still do now. I guess my mechanical phase is still going strong!

I really enjoy the water. I've spent time on it and under it, sailing and scuba diving. The water is a great teacher. You learn quickly to respect Her! In my water phase, I frustrated Dad yet again; he got me an electric trolling motor for a boat I built, and I modified the motor to pull me around underwater. He wasn't thrilled. Still, there is really nothing like zooming around almost effortlessly just above the seabed, and I could propel the boat with oars or a sail. Even though I seldom make time now to be on the water, it's good to be able to see Her and keep that connection alive. That's another lifelong phase!

Of course, there are phases we go through that are not of our making. I suppose potty training and learning to walk were some early, short phases. Getting through grade school is another, somewhat longer, phase. Attempting to become socially adept is another long phase for me, and I've never quite mastered it. Then there's college, or maybe professional training, as a prerequisite for getting along in our society. I couldn't wait to get out of school. I was lucky to have a handful of great teachers, but it sure felt good to relearn how much fun learning could be once I was doing it on my own. I hope that I never feel so old that learning loses its appeal!

At this end of my life, maybe I've entered a reflective phase. I like to be able to put together what I see, feel, imagine, and know to create a tapestry, so that I get an idea of how the world is woven together and how we are all part of that cloth. Most of my life, I've looked for patterns. This bigger tapestry could be a much larger pattern, one that helps me understand how our world is put together, and what our place in it is.

If it Looks Like Magic, You Don't Understand it Well Enough

That may sound harsh, but it's hard to argue the truth of it. Actually, there is **plenty** I don't understand... What **is** gravity? Where is all that "black matter " we hear about?... What forces **really** shape our world? All these things might look like magic, but that just means there's more to explore.

History gives us good lessons here. Just one example was that Copernicus bucked the Church when he suggested that the sun was the center of our solar system, rather than the Earth. Astrologers, astronomers, and mathematicians were all thought to be roughly the same profession in the 1500s, so it's not hard to imagine how difficult it was to actually figure out what was happening in the night sky. They all were simply confused in their understanding of planetary motion, and the Church doesn't tend to accept new theories quickly. Copernicus got free of the problem by dying.

Imagine someone from the 1920s watching our daily lives. Computer, what's that? Going down the road in your car at seventy mph, that's crazy—it'll suck the air right out of you! Cell phones are magic boxes that perform all kinds of tricks. The folks from 1920 might have remembered using covered wagons to cross the U.S., so flying in a jet—making the same trip in hours—would seem miraculous, too. All these things are common to us and hold little magic, particularly when going through security at an airport, but these days we understand the basics of what they do and how.

But there is still much we don't understand in the universe. My uneducated guess is that we'd be doing quite well if we understood 10% of what there is to know. But, realistically, we probably understand much less than that. For example, how do the animals and plants communicate? We have evidence that they do, but how? What's inside of a black hole—and, if we went there, how would we let humanity know what we found?

But we keep on expanding our knowledge base. I enjoyed studying dinosaurs when I was a kid. What we know about them now is much different and far richer. Once, germs were just theoretical. Now we take their existence as a given. Perhaps someday we'll be able to look at the structures of atoms the way we now look at bacteria under a microscope. It will just be a fancier microscope!

Our understanding of things grows with effort and time, and there is a **lot** to keep track of to stay current. Unfortunately, we need to accept that our minds are limited in capacity, and I wonder what we have given up in order to be able to hold all of this modern science and busy world in our brains. To contrast, ancient man seemed to be far better connected to the natural environment than we are. Have we lost that magic because our mind space is taken up with modern stuff? Certainly, there is a balance to be found so we can keep the best of both worlds.

A story is told that, when Europeans first came to the Americas, the Natives simply could not see the ships with billowing sails because they had nothing in their experience to help them make sense of the ships' appearance. If this is true, it makes me wonder about what we're able to see today and what we miss. Are we surrounded by aliens, but just can't see them and their technology because it's vastly different from us and ours? Is there even a way to answer that question with what we do know?

My purpose in writing all this isn't to confuse or to put what we do know in a bad light. It's to ask questions that might open our minds to the universe of possibilities for learning, and to help our minds stay open to strange and unimagined possibilities. After all, magic is an enticement to understand better and to explore. One definition of it is simply, "wonderful: exciting." That makes it sound like we're on an adventure, looking for the secrets of our universe and beyond!

Taking the Long View

All in all, 2020 was a pretty yucky year. Everybody knew about the virus and the useless politics. At the time I wrote this, over 320,000 people in the U.S. had died of SARS-CoV-2, and when this book published that number had grown to over one million deaths in the U.S. alone, with over six million deaths worldwide— yet the political scene allowed and even promoted ignoring science. As a result, the likelihood is that the virus will be around for a very long time, because we keep spreading it and giving it a chance to mutate and evade existing treatments, even three years after the pandemic began.

As if all that weren't enough, fires were ravaging the state of California, where I live. I had to evacuate that autumn, not knowing if I'd have a home to return to. (In a slightly twisted bit of fortune, evacuating was less difficult than it might have been because I had moved my disabled wife out of the house to be closer to a hospital and better care. So she was safe, away from the fire.) When the smoke cleared, I was lucky; I still have the home I built. Many others don't have theirs anymore.

Still, being that close to a destructive wildfire caused stress for me and others around me, even the animals. Cats like knowing their territory and need familiar surroundings. I had to move my cats to a safer place, where they were crammed into one room for most of a week. All four cats demonstrated the effects of the stress in different ways. The two young ones, Prince and Loca, used to be pretty even-keeled, but now they're scared of me during the day and only willing to be sort of social at night. One of the older cats, Shadow, started licking himself so much that bare spots developed.

The other older cat, Rex, developed serious digestive problems from the stress. The vet thought we had figured it out, but my cat went into shock from it and could not be saved. I had raised both older cats from small kittenhood, When Rex and Shadow together could fit easily in one hand. I bottle-fed them and we bonded. Shadow would follow me around like a dog. Rex would start purring if I just looked at him. We had all the signals worked out. I could give them direction, or they could let me know what they wanted. They were my kids in a very real way.

Writing about losing Rex was difficult for me. That's why I titled this piece "Taking the Long View." I'm hoping that a long perspective will help me make the transition from how it was to how it is. I knew a woman who lost her young adult son; it took her about five years to regain any sense of normalcy. I had no idea how long it would take before I felt normal once Rex was gone. With that, on top of the pandemic and the country going mad, I was not about to ask what else could go wrong. The universe can get creative that way.

I wrote this piece so that I could get it out and down in writing, so I wouldn't have to carry it around quite so much. I hoped that writing this would guide me to that longer view, and I'm hoping that view now has some peace and stillness in it. Those would be healing.

About a week had passed, and I was still missing Rex a lot. My cats get to name themselves, and Rex called himself The King. He acted royal from the start. He was almost never scared. He expected his human to take care of things as needed, and to make sure that His Royalness was always satisfied. He was nearly always kind to others (cats and humans), but should you cross a line, he'd let you know where your place was. He was also trusting, letting me carry him around upside down. Most felines don't tolerate that sort of behavior from their humans.

▲▲▲

After months had passed, I still felt Rex's loss lurking right below the surface. Rex's brother, Shadow, was making it hard to type as he sat on my lap. He seemed to need a lot of attention after Rex left, and he got it.

We don't have much choice but to adjust and keep on living after loss, trying to remember the good stuff that came from knowing the friends, relatives, and pets who have left us. I rationalize that having had them in my life has made me richer in many ways, and there is no denying that truth. I have learned that avoiding or denying the pain of loss only makes you hurt longer. Also, I get satisfaction from carrying those who have left around with me, remembering to be and do what would make them smile, purr, or wag their tails. It brings a nice measure of balance to living in a crazy time.

Quotations

I can't help it; I'm just **"** drawn to quotations. Can't get enough of them. To me, they are the distilled wisdom (and sometimes craziness) of humanity since the beginning of written language—around 6,000 years ago. Guesstimates are that we've had spoken

language for 50,000 to 100,000 years. With luck, some of that earlier wisdom has also come through into writing!

I once spent a week on my couch at home, just reading quotations. My excuse was that I was writing a book, and I wanted quotations throughout to make it more interesting. After all, it was a book on water heaters, so anything to make it more readable was appreciated! Also, you can say things via quotations from others that you could never say directly. And the right quotation at the bottom of a page can convey good stuff! I figure that I read about 30,000 quotes that week, and it was easily the best vacation I ever had. My mind soared high at times, or found unexpected humor, or simply was able to clearly see connections between the distant past and right now. I wouldn't have been surprised if you had walked in and told me that I was floating a few inches off the couch. It was **that** good!

Of course, there are all kinds of quotations. Some are just funny or silly, but the ones I like best bring out truth in a new light or perspective. Truth is hard to be certain about sometimes, so anything that lets me get a grasp on it is my friend. Knowing and using truth gives one a firm place to stand, and that really matters, particularly in difficult times. This may be my favorite quote on truth:

The inquiry of truth, which is the love-making, or the wooing of it, the knowledge of truth, which is the presence of it, and the belief of truth, which is the enjoying of it, is the sovereign good of human nature.

That's from Francis Bacon, who was born in 1560. It seems he was a smart guy and had a lot to say about truth, which makes me suspect that it was important to him. I pondered that quotation for well over an hour before truly getting it. It washed over me in waves.

Truth is no less important these days, when we are flooded with so much information and misinformation. The year 2020 had just finished when I was writing this piece, and certainly those could be called difficult times. If history has a lesson for us, it's that truth is even more important for our survival and sanity in difficult times. We had the maskers and the anti-maskers. We had the left and the right—and nobody, it seems, in the middle. We had fear, greed, and inequality when we needed to be focused on the common good, and the greater good. To me, these were all reasons to slow down and read some quotations! Quotations can bring us perspective and balance. Regaining those important tools will help us understand where we are, and lead us to see the interconnectedness of all living things.

I'd like to tell you about my favorite book of quotations so that you might sit down with it and have a wonderful, useful time. It's called

The Great Quotations, and was put together by George Seldes. From the back cover:

> Many great ideas are controversial. With courage and conviction Mr. Seldes has compiled a vital selection of these controversial ideas—of the words and thoughts that have moved mankind. *The Great Quotations* is a brilliant wellspring for all who seek to enlighten, encourage, persuade, or to inspire.

That pretty well sums up my feelings.

I just had a look at my favorite used book search site, www.addall.com, and found *The Great Quotations* for as little as $1.50 plus shipping. That's a pretty inexpensive way to hold onto your sanity in any difficult times!

Out There

Imagine

Imagine living our very best lives. It wouldn't be just getting by or making do, but really living to our fullest potential. What would that be like and how would we get there? I can only make wild guesses, but clearly, three huge impediments exist that seriously  get in the way of having our best lives. They are connectedness, health, and fear. Let's examine them a bit closer.

Look at where we are now, well past the Industrial Revolution, which finished up about 150 years ago (1790-1870). Because of our inventiveness, we're no longer all that well connected to the world around us. We live in big or little boxes we call homes, and we get around in smaller boxes we call cars. We taste and smell stuff, some of which our ancestors wouldn't have recognized as food. We listen to sounds from speakers and see images on little or big screens. We're well insulated and isolated from the rest of the natural world most of the time. I looked it up: We spend eighty-seven percent of our time indoors and six percent in our cars. That leaves seven percent of our time for getting in touch with the real world around us. Hmmm. Where did our species evolve? Outdoors! From having been outdoors nearly all of the time, now down to seven percent of the time, it makes me wonder if our psychology and physiology might have a bit of difficulty evolving and adapting.

Think about our health for a moment. We use allopathy, known as
Western medicine, which became widespread in the early 1800s (hmm,
much like the Industrial Revolution). It treats physical symptoms, and
less often treats the cause of a problem. Older systems of medicine, like
Ayurveda, Traditional Chinese, Greek, Roman, and Native American,
look at physical, mental, and spiritual conditions, and have been around
roughly twenty times as long. Also, these older sciences go after the root
causes of disease rather than just the symptoms. I boil it down like this:
prevention vs. reaction = traditional medicine vs. Western medicine. I
do think Western medicine has its place but we damage ourselves by
ignoring all the other kinds of medicine. An example of this is cancer.
In the U.S., we cut out the tumor and take poison to keep the cancer at
bay. Why aren't we looking for what caused the cancer in the first place
so that we can truly be cured?

Think about what life was like before the Industrial Revolution and
Western medicine. Native Americans, Aborigines, and all other ancient
civilizations didn't have the option of being unaware of the natural
world. If they didn't pay attention—and closely—they would die an early
death from lack of food or by becoming a meal for some other animal.
All of their "medicine" came from the great outdoors. They had a deep
understanding and intense perception of the world around them that
we generally lack today. Simply put, they saw and understood stuff that
is still there, which we don't notice now.

Indigenous people were tuned in to the worlds of animal and plant
life. Animal communication, which is considered strange and rare today,
seems to have been widely understood and accepted by past, less frenetic
civilizations. It's not hard to find people today who are practiced in
animal communication, and they have some amazing stories to tell.
I think my favorite story is about Anna Breytenbach and Spirit, the
black leopard. She was able to sit with the leopard and understand his
perspective and concerns. From there, she was able to give the leopard
assurances that he would suffer no more abuse or demands upon him.
The leopard's demeanor changed instantly from angry to content, and has

remained so. It may seem like magic, but the results of communicating with animals are hard to deny.

In order to communicate with animals, it seems that one's ability to really quiet one's mind is important. Ms. Breytenbach suggests that communication happens on a quantum level; it's like a phone line that all of life uses. Only humans—with our preoccupied, noisy minds—have forgotten how to be in touch with other species. It probably shouldn't be surprising that our ancestors, who were so nicely tuned into the world around them, seem to have been able to communicate with other species as if it were the most natural thing to do. Wouldn't it be amazing to tune in to redwood trees and get their perspective? A tree might be surprised that you didn't come with a saw, but came to quietly listen and have a conversation.

Robin Wall Kimmerer (author of *Braiding Sweetgrass)* has proposed that we banish the word "it" from our vocabulary when referring to plants and animals, and substitute the word "kin," asserting that all other life forms are kinfolk. By reducing other beings to a simple "it," our language encourages us to disrespect other life.

I'd like to add to this discussion a big one: fear. Fear can be a huge noisemaker in our heads. So much of what we do, how we see the world, and how we think is based on fear...

"What if we have no money?"

"That person is different than I am. I don't know what he'll do, so he's scary!"

"I have money and possessions, so others will try to take them. I must protect myself from all of those takers."

How can we hope to connect with the world around and in us when we're seeing the world through fear-colored glasses?

Fear is mostly a projection. It's about what could happen in some unhappy future. Even when you're comfortable in a safe and secure place, it's easy to be scared. And how often do those bad things we worry about actually happen? I'm not saying you should be unaware of things that could go badly, but rather I suggest that we go slowly, prepare, and be ready instead of worried. Imagine what a life without fear and worry would feel like. Not bad, huh? Also, it's pretty clear that fear is used as a tool to control how we act. The IRS uses it, and I imagine lots of others do, too. There are plenty of sticks and not enough carrots! So imagine the freedom that having no fear could bring. Try pondering how you would live your life differently without it.

Think a bit about these three topics—connectedness, health, and fear. If we were in close touch with our living world, so we never experienced loneliness and had a greater understanding of "kin"; if we were in great health, living long and satisfying lives; and if fear had no toehold, but rather peacefulness was the norm, wouldn't that be a wonderful existence? All we need now is to imagine how to get there!

Protection

Have you ever felt protected? Years ago, I was driving down a winding, rural, two-lane road in the late afternoon. It had just rained and there was no wind. I was driving at the speed limit and there was oncoming traffic. Next to the road was an old oak tree. The weight of the rainwater on that tree was just a bit too much  for it to bear, so with no warning, the sky above me turned green…and I was driving my old Dodge pickup right through the falling tree.

I had seen the trunk of a large tree just past that falling oak, so I aimed toward where memory told me was a safe place, at the side of the road. My truck came to a stop about six feet from that tree trunk. I began to take stock. It looked like a bomb had gone off in the cab of my truck. The roof support was bent and the windshield was half gone. The passenger-side fender was smashed into the tire, and even the truck bed had a big dent in it.

But interestingly, the windshield went missing in a strange way. There was a line right down the center of it. On the passenger side, there was no glass left at all, but on my side the glass was just fine—not even a crack in it. The passenger seat was sprayed with glass bits, but my side was clean. I didn't know what to think or feel.

A woman came running down from a nearby house and asked if I was OK, giving me a hug. I really didn't know. She looked me over for blood or damage and found none. I was completely unscathed!

Years later, I met the guy who'd been driving in the opposite direction when the oak fell. He told me that he'd seen an oak tree down on the road (even into his lane)—then a truck came flying out of the tree a few feet off the ground! Guess we both got surprised that day.

That story confirmed my sense that I'd been protected when that big oak fell, and I was grateful, but couldn't help but wonder what I'd been saved for. Since I'd so clearly been saved (I can still see that oddly broken windshield in my mind), what were the greater plans and what was my role in them?

I seem to be a fairly spiritual guy, and have felt connected to the living world most of my life, so the notion that I must have a purpose doesn't feel strange. I'm not into the "live just to suffer and die" thing. I do like, and actually need, to be helpful, and am happy to do it invisibly. Recognition doesn't matter.

Just living day to day can feel like a story without a plot. But being protected gives a bigger context. It gives me guidance and a reason for being here, along with some confidence and stability. It lets me be even-keeled, even in a storm. My life's story has a plot! So, just maybe, I was protected so that I could encourage, help, and protect all other life. It's just a hunch, but that's enough for me.

Acceptance Land

You may have heard of Shangri-La, a mythical place of peace and beauty. In many ways, Acceptance Land (AL) is similar to Shangri-La, but for one very important difference. It's real! Like Shangri-La, it is amazingly difficult to find, but once you have made the journey, you'll be able to get there whenever you wish. AL truly is a special place. When you're there, you'll notice that people are not judged on their clothes, or the color of their skin, or their skill with social circumstances. In fact, they are simply not judged! Carrying judgment around is not a burden the residents of AL choose to have on their backs or minds. They

choose to look at facts, discern the intentions of others, and then be guided by those things.

AL also has guiding lights. The truth there is not so flexible, as it can be elsewhere. In AL they all work from the same facts and the same truths, which remain solid and unchanging over time. And they are always on the lookout for new or undiscovered truths. Imagine if we could do that here. So much dissent would simply fade away as it would have nothing to stand on. One other big difference is that in AL, there is no fear because there is nothing to be afraid of. In AL, fear isn't a habit. The residents support each other, and help all other life forms. They feel they are part of a larger web of life and treat it with respect. There is no need to amass money or lots of stuff in AL, as there is no risk of scarcity or need for power over anybody or anything. After all, it IS a special place. Even the concept of death, which many find scary here, is to the residents of AL simply a transition. It can be a joyful change, because you'll get to visit an unknown realm and learn new things while leaving that old, worn-out body behind.

AL is clearly a rare and wonderful place...but how to find it? The discovery of AL seems to be one of those instances where the truth hides in plain sight. In order to see the path, we need the right eyes. Okay, so how do we get that kind of vision? Let's take this in small steps. We know that AL harbors no fear, so let's try practicing getting rid of fear as a response to events around us. Let's drop all the luggage that fear creates and see if the path to AL becomes a bit more apparent. Let's skip judgment and the separation it always creates. This encourages unity and a feeling of connectedness. It can even empower love, which casts a light that no unhappy force can dim. Fear and hate must flee from love, which just happens to be the coin of the realm rather than empty money. With love there can be no scarcity or judgment. Does a mother judge her baby, or simply pour on the love?

So, are you beginning to feel what it's like to be in AL? Good! Now go have a look in the mirror. Take your time and look deeply. Acceptance Land is right in front of you. You know the path to this magnificent place, and can be there anytime you want!

 Look for balance between good and bad, light and dark, love and fear.

If Everyone Were Just Like Me...Musing in a Seussian Sort of Way

If everyone were just like me, wouldn't that be wonderful to see? Imagine how great life would be if we all had the same point of view—and if we always knew just how and who others would be? No upset or surprise, because we'd all have just the same amount of wise.
How great would it be if you were just like me, and I was just like you? We'd have fun. We'd find things to do! We all could be one vast flock, happy in our sameness, solid as a rock. There would be no need to name

us, just plenty of sameness. And anyone could be leavin' with no hurt feelin'. Imagine how peaceful it would be, not having to hear unusual thoughts or disturbing ideas? Could it be, or am I talking panaceas?

Yup, it sure would be sweet to be so alike, no different thoughts, headed down the same turnpike. We'd turn in unison, just like a school of fish, identical in every way, as we think we wish. Those old ideas of being independent and unique, well, they are only for the old antique. What joy could possibly come of difference, when we're pretty sure anything else is of no consequence? Some may long for the bad old days, when people thought for themselves, but isn't that really sort of a haze? It's pleasanter to skip that thinking stuff and happily look at you, or into the mirror as we're all the same. And being the same, why we wouldn't even need to have names. Plain the same. And as long as we're on it, what good are feelings? Feelin' just makes us think about bein' and that's sure a bunch of work, buzzin' around! So smug in our sameness we could be, with none of that boring individuality. What is this living for anyway? When we're dead, now that's a great place, cuz then we'll all be going just the same pace. Yup!

So, I've been tinking bout dis a bit more, and lately and it comes to me: I may a been just a bit hasty. I mean, so what if you're different than me? Isn't that really how we're all meant to be? You know what the French say, "Viva la Difference!" Well, that may just make some sense. Part of the beauty in a sunset is that you never know what you'll get. They change minute by minute if you've got time to stick with it. So, even with some adversity, the world is a fine place to be with all of its diversity. I think I'll stop while I'm ahead, and maybe go to bed…and pet a cat!

 Listen closely to your hunches and gut feelings. They can be lifesaving.

How Ya Doin'?

What comes to mind when someone asks you that question? Do you think of what's right? What's wrong? Or a mixture of both? My experience is that most people tend to focus on what they think needs work, or what's missing from their lives. Some recite a list  of things that need doing, or their health issues, or people problems. It's almost considered a joke that when "old" people get together, they talk about their aches and pains, competing for the prize of who feels worst.

FYI, I tried being a cynic for a while and it just didn't pay. Going out of my way to see what was wrong, and how others could have done better, just put me into a pretty deep hole. So I chose optimism. It's a far nicer path to be on.

I'm wondering if simply demonstrating care might sometimes be better than asking how you're doing. If I do a good deed for you, or bring a gift—even if it's simply a smile—isn't it likely to help you feel cared about without opening the door to feeling bad about what's wrong with your life? Hmmm…

So, how do we get used to seeing what's right and lose the focus on what's wrong? One way to focus on what's going right is to practice gratitude. Gratitude is defined as "the quality of being thankful; readiness to show appreciation for and to return kindness."

But look at what feeling grateful does. It makes you notice things that are right with your world—just the opposite of noticing what's wrong. Being aware of what's right and noticing what we can be thankful for feel like a perfect counterpoint to these times of pandemic and turmoil.

How do we create more gratitude in our lives? I've noticed that if I do something good for others, something good always happens for me. I never know where that good thing will come from, but it always—and

I do mean always—comes. This isn't why I do good things for others; I just like doing them! I like seeing the smile and the look of wonder on their faces. Or, when I do something nice without their knowing or ever learning that I did it, I like to imagine that they felt the universe was watching out for them. For me, being helpful is a two-for-one. I get to see happy results, and something good always happens for me. How could I **not** be grateful?

I'll add that "helping" is one good reason to never stop learning. When you know stuff, you can use it to help. A better life happens for you and those around you when helping is a way of life. Have you ever rescued someone from a threatening situation? When you have helped, gratitude naturally follows. You feel good that you were in a position to make a real difference. That positivity even helps us to be healthier and live longer!

By the way, that rabbit in the photo is no ordinary rabbit. He has a lesson for us. He's a suburban Long Island Rabbit and is quite comfortable, even around cars and concrete. He knows what's right! So, if you ask him how things are, he'll probably just raise an eyebrow and keep on having somebody's lawn for lunch, wondering why you asked a question with such an obvious answer. He's having a free and tasty lunch in his hometown. What could be better? Turns out rabbits understand English but don't care to speak it. Sometimes it can be difficult to see when a rabbit from the burbs raises an eyebrow. You must watch very closely! 😉

So now, when a good friend asks, "How are ya now?" I don't have to sort between the light and the dark; I just pet the cat a bit more, or remember to notice the great view, and say, "Things are good, thanks. How 'bout you?"

What is the Value of Life?

I was outside splitting logs for the wood stove. I use a little hand-powered log splitter to do this. As I was splitting a log, the bark slid back and exposed a moth, unhurt, but clearly not in a good place. I gently picked up the moth and put it on a tarp close by. But it had rained earlier, and I unwittingly put the moth in a little pool of clear rainwater! I quickly scooped him out and placed him properly on a dry spot. He folded his wings, just so, and was fine despite my ineptitude.

Is old age making me silly, so that I care about the life of a common moth? As a child, I remember watching cartoons in which the crazy old guy would go out of his way to avoid stepping on ants marching in a line on the sidewalk. That was considered to be a loony-tune activity. I also remember thinking he had good eyes!

Recently, I've been reading a book called *Braiding Sweetgrass*. The author makes a point that our language turns non-human beings into "its." You wouldn't call your grandmother "it!" It is in the kitchen, making us all dinner! She suggests that our language trains our minds to diminish other living beings. It's pretty easy to take the life of an "it," but not so easy with a "he" or a "she." Our language allows us to see nearly everything that isn't human as a resource to be used—and used up—rather than as living beings who give to us, and who need to be helped and treated with respect so that we make our entire world healthier and stronger by our presence.

I don't know what it's like to live the life of a moth. It might be just fabulous when you're not being dunked in water! Or it might be fraught with difficulties and challenges, just as our lives are. But this line of thought raises a question: Why is "life, liberty, and the pursuit of happiness" only for humans? If there were a being on Earth who was so big and so powerful that we could not comprehend any way to influence his or her actions, and if this being seemingly randomly went around killing us and crushing our towns, wouldn't we feel somewhat less than satisfied? Imagine, now, how other species might see the presence of modern humanity on the Earth: Ancient trees are for cutting; animals are for hunting or slaughtering; forests are for cutting down and turning into farmland, eliminating diversity. None of these other species has the tools to fight back; if they did, you can be sure they would.

I've come to believe that all of life is entitled to being lived well, no matter who that life belongs to. Although I'm a vegetarian, this isn't a diatribe against eating meat or anything along those lines, or how it relates to making different choices for ourselves. It's about seeing a bigger picture and being respectful of all living beings. If you need to take another's life to keep your own going, please do it respectfully and with reciprocity. "Reciprocity" means that, if you are taking something, find a way to give back. Keeping our systems in balance matters. Otherwise, we're simply spoiling our own nest, which probably won't work out nicely in the long run for any form of life here. We are part of the larger web of life, and if we don't value all of life, we ourselves are damaged. Ultimately, we humans can only benefit by being good stewards of our living planet.

So, to answer the title question, the value of life is in living it. Everything we can do to help all beings live their best and fullest life enrichens our own. There is an ancient Hindu term, Namaste, which means "the sacred in me recognizes the sacred in you." It is commonly understood that life is sacred. There's the value of life!

 Make truth your goddess. She's powerful, giving, and so wise.